T0090339

Also by Tom Groneberg

The Secret Life of Cowboys

One Good Horse

★　★　★

Tom Groneberg

SCRIBNER
New York　London　Toronto　Sydney

SCRIBNER
1230 Avenue of the Americas
New York, NY 10020

SCRIBNER and design are trademarks of Macmillan Library Reference USA, Inc.,
used under license by Simon & Schuster, the publisher of this work.

For information about special discounts for bulk purchases,
please contact Simon & Schuster Special Sales:
1-800-456-6798 or business@simonandschuster.com

DESIGNED BY ERICH HOBBING

Text set in Garamond #3

Manufactured in the United States of America

1   3   5   7   9   10   8   6   4   2

Library of Congress Cataloging-in-Publication Data

Groneberg, Tom, 1966–
One good horse / Tom Groneberg.
p. cm.
1. Horses—Montana. 2. Horses—Training—Montana.
3. Ranch life—Montana. 4. Groneberg, Tom, 1966– I. Title.
SF301.G76 2006
636.1'0835—dc22
2005054112

ISBN-13: 978-0-7432-6518-8
ISBN-10: 0-7432-6518-1

To Jennifer, always
And to Mr. Forrest Davis, Bronco Bob Ricketts,
Blue, and the Boys

One Good Horse

Preface

In trots the colt. Look at him. Beautiful and nameless. A coming two-year-old. His black mane traps the sunlight, his coat still shaggy from winter. Eyes bright, mischievous, like a little boy waiting to pull a trick. Like me, he is full of wonder and a little scared. He trots around the small round corral, showing off a bit, kicking at a cloud. And then he stops and turns toward me, breathing me in. Waiting. Waiting for the heavy spring clouds to lift and reveal the heights of the Mission Mountains. Waiting for the shadows of returning birds to paint the land gray. I remember how the lake, now like poured lead, turns summer chrome. I remember it all, sometimes, just before I go to bed.

Memory is a narcotic. The outstretched arms of a souvenir as it beckons you to remember, to dream. In this life, you are promised nothing, and everything.

I look back sometimes, and though I recall vague out-

1

lines, I cannot remember the specific shape of things that were once so important in my life. A boss's face, the sound of a cast-iron triangle calling wranglers and sleepy-eyed dudes to breakfast in an aspen-gold Colorado meadow, the way the bottom of a horse's hoof looks like a charcoal heart. In my twenties, I fell in love. Everything happened so fast, I'm not sure what I fell in love with first: the horse, the girl, or the land. I know for certain I loved the girl the most and that everything good flowed from that love. After we graduated from college, Jennifer and I moved west together, searching for a life to call our own. Two years later, we were married. Another five years found us on a ranch in southeastern Montana, fifteen square miles of shortgrass and sagebrush and space that I never could contain, no matter how much fence I built. The ranch failed me, and I failed the ranch. Running the place was more than I could manage, like some anxiety nightmare, a test I couldn't pass. And I thought that having to sell out and leave those dreams behind was the break in my heart that I would nurse the rest of my life. We were just beginning to talk about having kids, about starting our family. Carter was born on New Year's Eve, six years ago. It seems only a hoofbeat ago, a lifetime.

New Year's Eve. It's a good time to look forward and back and try to see how far you've come. I write Carter letters to try to capture time, to hold it for a while, with words. There is so much I want to tell him, so many things I want to say. Balancing between this year and last, I can't remember what I've written in the past. I imagine, read back to back, the letters pin me down as a repetitive old man, a bore spouting the same stale stories about the state of the world and our little place in it. What I'm really trying to do is to tell Carter how much I love him and his mother, to make up for all of the times I've forgotten to say it out loud. Now, I can't imagine there is anything left to say. Or, maybe, there is too much. I know it won't fit on a page or two, won't wait for the day when my son opens the wrinkled envelopes and smoothes each page, the years unfolding.

When Carter tries to tell a story and it all comes out at once and he gulps air like he is drowning in words, Jennifer tells him, "Do your best. Use your words. Go slow." I am not too proud to take advice meant for a little boy.

Use words.

Go slow.

Slower still.

Chapter One

INVENTING A STORY WITH GRASS,
I FIND A YOUNG HORSE DEEP INSIDE IT.
—JAMES DICKEY,
"A Birth"

The autumn moon rises full and blue and marbled over the Mission Valley. In a barn, at the end of a lane, the mare grunts, lies on her side, stands, lies back down. The man is there, watching from the shadows, his rough hands ready to go to work if there are any problems. His son, Clay, stands alongside in all his red silence. After thirty minutes of labor, the slick black narrow thing slips into the straw of the stall. The mare looks over her shoulder, nuzzles the foal, then rocks to her feet. The man nods, says "That's a girl," and heads back into the house for some fresh coffee, copper-haired Clay trailing behind.

The colt looks even blacker when it begins to snow a month later. Winter settles into the valley, the snow falling everywhere. The colt nuzzles his mother, her milk warming his belly. She shelters him from the wind when it blows cold and wet from the lake. On New Year's Eve, fireworks shotgun the midnight sky. The colt looks up at the bright sparks falling, falling. He is now able to run circles around the small pasture by the barn without slipping from the slick snow and from his own young clumsiness.

When there is nothing but April mud left in the pasture, the men move the colt, his mother, and the other mares and foals across the highway to the big field alongside the lake.

In May, the swampy ground is a riot of sweet clover and sego lilies, skunk cabbage, and cattails. The colt seems to grow with the sun, from the moment its light breaks across the tops of the mountains to the east. Rampant and wild, he runs with his little brush of a tail held high, shaking his head and kicking at nothing.

By late July, the colt is all knees and nose, a coming yearling. The men call him Black, though he isn't as black as when he was first born. He spends most of his waking hours grazing, his front feet spread wide so he can reach the low grass. And though he's weaned from her, the colt often stands alongside the mare, a shadow of her, watching the other horses, watching the clouds above and the wind in the cottonwood trees.

The grass didn't have much of a chance to grow this year, and some of the horses stand, gaunt and ribby, in the fading summer light. It never got so bad that the sheriff had to come out and inspect the horses for abuse, but there was talk. Some called it horse hoarding, having too many animals to care for. Others just called it bad luck.

Early one morning, four men ride through the pasture

on horseback. They push the loose horses to the small barbed-wire enclosure in the southeast corner of the field, where another man spreads hay on the bare ground, calling out, "Hey, hay." The herd moves to the pen, strung out in a long line of horses of different colors and sizes. Brown-and-white paints, a black Thoroughbred, the blue roan. Most of the mares are bred, with foals at their sides. Some of the older horses are lame and defeated, limping after the younger, fitter horses. Once the herd is gathered from the big pasture, the men on horseback listen as the man on foot tells them which horses to turn back out. "That big paint goes," he calls out, pointing, "and that buckskin and the black colt." In all, forty horses are turned back into the big pasture and the wire gate is closed. The hundred head that remain are pushed, ten at a time, into the wooden pen. The men use stock whips and nylon ropes and swear words to load five horses into each trailer. Diesel engines idling. Hoppers practicing their grass dance at the men's feet.

Once the horses are loaded, they are driven sixty miles north to the auction yard in Kalispell. They are sold on a Wednesday. Old and young, the paints, the Thorough-breds, registered and grade. They sell for next to nothing, run through the ring without saddle or sales pitch. Most are bound for the cannery.

Back home, the not-so-black colt clips the scant dry grass with his twelve milk teeth, not knowing the fate of his siblings or his mother or himself. Knowing only grass and light.

September, and my in-laws are visiting from Chicago. After dinner, my father-in-law, Fred, and I drive to the little bar and restaurant out on the highway for a drink, maybe a quiet game of pool. It's a rural Montana bar that caters to fishermen and construction workers and retirees. Huge lake trout hang, stuffed and mounted, along the upper reaches of the walls. Below, vintage fishing poles and treble-hooked lures are nailed alongside framed photographs of volunteer fire department picnics taken long before I joined the department. It's the perfect place for some conversation and a beer or two. But when we get there, the parking lot is full.

"Friday night," Fred says.

But even so, the bar is rarely ever crowded. I pull across the highway and park my truck in front of the fire hall. "You don't have to lock it," I tell Fred. We walk across the pavement to the bar. "I've never seen it this busy."

Inside, a small sound system has been set up in front of the short wall of video poker and keno machines. It's karaoke night. A three-ring binder filled with song lyrics passes from hand to hand. Fred buys us the first round and, as he hands me the bottle, he says, "They tried to put an olive in my beer."

"Local custom," I say. "Cheers." We clink our bottles together and find a place to watch and listen. First, a woman does her best to channel Mariah Carey. Next, a nervous college kid tries to imitate Bob Dylan. After a brief break, two men stand there, microphones in hand. I recognize the shorter one, he works at the bank in town. But the other man is a stranger to me. He has a full mustache and is wearing a black felt cowboy hat, Wranglers, and leather boots. The music to a Righteous Brothers song begins. The soundtrack swells, the bar noise quiets, and for a moment the cowboy's voice rises above us all. It's so beautiful and sad that, even in the hot, crowded bar, I feel a little chill. And then it is over.

Fred leans in close. "Who's that?"

I shrug. "Don't know."

The man running the sound equipment looks like a stand-in for Burt Reynolds. He picks up a microphone and says, "We'll take a short break and have some more karaoke fun in fifteen minutes."

Fred and I finish our beers and I get us another round. "Who was that singing?" I ask the bartender. "The one with the cowboy hat?"

"That's Bob Dog," he says. "Runs Three Dog Down. You want olives with these?"

"No, thanks." I hand Fred his beer and say, "That cowboy runs a place that sells down comforters on the edge of town." And, since the music has stopped and my tongue is loosened by the beer, I tell Fred what's on my mind. "Jen and I have been thinking about getting you another grandchild, a little brother or a sister for Carter."

He smiles.

Fred is the father of two girls, so I hope he can reassure me that another child won't ruin Carter's world.

Fred says, "Don't worry. You won't have to share the love you have for Carter with another child. Your love grows."

I nod. It's what I wanted to hear, but still, I'm skeptical.

I think about love's ability to expand. I imagine a red balloon. A baby growing inside Jennifer. I picture more balloons, some are baby blue, others pink. Labor and birth, our family getting larger. I imagine balloons of all colors floating above the dining room table, which is loaded with presents, bowls of ice cream, and a large cake. I can hear my own voice, mouthing the words to someone else's song, as the flames on the candles dance.

"Here's to more kids," Fred says, raising his beer in a toast. I take a long, deep drink. And then Fred says quietly, "God, he had a beautiful voice."

The colt has always stood out among the other young horses, for no other reason than he was born in the fall. He is fourteen months old, now, still intact and unbranded, smaller than the two-year-olds but larger than the yearlings.

The dark green flatbed truck makes its way up the gravel road to the wire gate that encloses fifty acres of frozen turf that was bared long ago. To the north, the pasture turns to willows and old cattails and lake and sky. To the south, a semitruck loaded with snow-covered logs speeds west on the highway, bound for the mill in Pablo.

The taller of the two men opens the passenger's-side door, gets out of the truck, and unlatches the wire gate, shooing horses from the opening as the other man drives through, then he climbs back into the truck. The truck bounces across frozen piles of manure, connecting the dots like constellations, then stops in the middle of the pasture.

The men get out and each grabs a wire-handled five-gallon plastic bucket filled with oats. They walk in opposite directions, pouring little piles of grain on the ground. There are bales of alfalfa to feed them as well, once the oats are gone. The taller man empties the last of his bucket. The horses crowd in. One of the older geldings bites a younger gray horse on the shoulder, to force him out of the way. The gray horse spins and pushes into the man, who swings his empty bucket at the horse, shouting, "Get off!" A hoof shoots out from the bunched horses and catches the tall man in the chest. He cries out and clutches his ribs and goes down, the bucket echoing as it bounces once on the hard ground. The other man drops his full bucket of oats and runs to help his brother up and into the truck. He drives to the wire gate, lays it down, drives across, then closes it. There is an urgency to his movements. The truck speeds down the gravel lane, turns west, and follows the highway toward town.

The dark brown colt stands over the spilled oats from the dropped bucket. His rear is to the other horses, and he eats greedily. Finally, the other horses gather around and the ground is licked clean in a matter of seconds.

Another January, and Carter and I have the run of the place, twenty-five hundred acres of land framed by the reach of the slate-colored Mission Mountains, their peaks buried in snow, the full blue span of the heavens above, the ground solid beneath our feet.

Phil, my boss, is spending two weeks in Mexico to

escape the gray crush of winter in northwest Montana. But today the clouds have disappeared and the sun is everywhere. Carter walks beside me with the energy of a small boy eager to help his father. He is fascinated with everything. The old barn, red and peeling in the sunlight. The overgrown apple orchard. The bales of hay stacked like toy blocks. Cows, sheep, chickens, mice. The horses. Like the current running though a single-wire electric fence, there is a hum to the place. It is life and it is death, but mainly it is life.

Jennifer is at a doctor's appointment. We've been trying to have another child for more than a year and now, she thinks she's pregnant. I wish I could be there, listening, asking questions, holding her hand, but I promised Phil I'd check the cows today. I also wish I could have spent time at home with Carter, reading picture books and drinking chocolate milk and eating cheddar-flavored goldfish crackers, since his days as an only child might be over soon. But instead we're here, and I feel that, despite my best efforts, I'm letting everyone down: Jennifer, Carter, my boss. I feel stretched too thin, and that is usually when bad things seem to happen.

The cows are grazing in a distant pasture, and the only way to get there is on the back of a horse. I grab a halter and a lead rope from the barn and head out to the small pasture in front of the house, Carter at my side. As we approach the hay feeders, the four ranch horses lift their heads and stare at us. The two younger ones, Dipper and Draco, begin moving toward the corral with an air of reluctant acceptance. I watch them, trying to decide which one to saddle. These are good solid horses, better than most, but still, I'm uneasy. There is no one around to hear us or to help us if something goes wrong. Between the front gate of the ranch and the front door of the small hospital in town, there are two miles of rutted gravel road and ten miles of pavement that take twenty minutes to cross, if you drive fast. But the greater distance would be the hundreds of acres of grass that we would need to cover on foot if something happened. The decision to ride one horse instead of the other could mean everything.

Carter wears his new helmet, a dome of plastic-covered Styrofoam decorated with black cows, white sheep, and pink pigs on a background of yellow and red. It looks fitted for this ranch work. His black fireman's helmet with the clear visor, the yellow hard hat with purple crayon marks, the ones for baseball and football, all of Carter's other helmets are just for play. This beautiful blond boy, in his first real helmet, breaks my heart. If something were to happen out here on the ranch, if Draco lost his footing on one of the steep hills or Dipper bolted at a flush of birds, the helmet wouldn't be enough to protect him. Carter stares down at an ancient cow pie lying at his feet, like a flattened brown hat in the grass, amazed at the amount of shit in the world.

Except for the star on Dipper's forehead, the horses look identical. Both are dark bays, quarter horses, equal in size and age. But there are slight differences between them. Dipper is more sure-footed. He pays attention when he is walking and doesn't stumble as often as Draco. But Draco is calmer, unlike Dipper, who takes off at the sight of Hungarian partridges lifting from the grass, as if he wants to join them in the sky. Since Carter will be riding in my lap, I decide to saddle Draco, the slow, even-tempered stumblebum.

As they walk toward the corral, Dipper and Draco are joined by Lad, a big, old, recently retired black horse. Like an old man who can't seem to hand over the family business to his son, Laddy still wants to work. He tags along and tries to be useful, but only ends up getting in the way. Spirit, the fourth horse, stands at the hay feeder, deflated and thin with age. His brown coat is rough and his black mane is in tangles. I love being able to share this with Carter, the horses and the cattle, green tractors and red barns, this life.

The air is remarkably still as the horses plod along ahead of us, a slow-moving progression of creaking joints and flatulence and sighs. Dipper is almost to the gate now, Draco and Lad following behind. It is a beautiful, common moment, one I hope will live on in my memory, and in Carter's memories of his childhood. Just as Dipper reaches the gate, he drops his head suddenly. He snorts, pivots, and runs back toward us, followed closely by Draco and Lad. I pull Carter to my side as the horses thunder past in an explosion of hooves and flying dirt. Carter and I stand motionless, his tiny hand in mine.

I think, perhaps for the first time, that I should have my own horse. If I walked out into a pasture with a halter, it would nicker and trot toward me. I wouldn't have to decide which horse to saddle, which animal to trust. If I had a good horse, I could give it my life. I could ride it for years. We could grow old together. Then I would give it to Carter. His own horse, to ride, to have, because I know I will not always be there for him.

I try to run the horses back to the corral, and Carter struggles to keep up. By now the sheep and the llama and a lump-jawed Hereford that share this small pasture are in the mix, darting here and there. I bite the inside of my mouth, trying to remain calm, trying not use the "Daddy words" Carter is fond of repeating.

"Just stand against the fence and watch," I say, but as I step away, the brown llama comes up behind Carter and scares him with its monkey face, its buck teeth, and black eyes.

"Camel!" Carter yells, holding back his sobs, trying not to show his fear.

I avert my gaze and wave my arms at the shaggy beast, because I once heard a llama will spit at you if you look it directly in the eye. It runs off and joins the sheep in the far corner of the pasture. I squat down and hug Carter.

"Let's stick together," I say. "I have another plan."

I lift Carter onto my shoulders. He gives a happy yell as I jog around the pasture, slipping in a fresh cow pie and nearly buckling to the ground. He grips me tighter, holding my chin with both hands, but then he lets go, just one hand clamped on my left ear. I see our shadow playing out on the yellow winter grass. Carter's free hand is in the air, rodeo style, waving at the heavens. He kicks me in the shoulders, spurring me, as I trot across the small pasture behind the three horses. The heels of his tiny snow boots dig into my sides, punching me, but I cannot bring myself to ask him to stop. Together, we move the animals into the corral and close the big green metal gate behind them.

Sometimes, when I'm lying in bed at night, unable to fall asleep, I play a game in my head, trying to recall the names of all of the horses I've known since moving west from Illinois. Of the seventy horses at the stables in Breckenridge, I remember Catch and Bandanna, Rebel and Ruby and Scout most clearly. At Calvin Brown's ranch in Niarada, the horses were nameless: the registered stud, the brood mares, and the doomed colt that was born blind. At Tim's ranch in Eureka, there was Sonny and Corky and Rip. Balty and Cagey, the two saddle horses on the place my family owned outside of Miles City. I try to remember them all, the many horses that have run in and out of my life over the last thirteen years. They carried me from paycheck to paycheck, from Colorado to the Canadian line.

Draco picks his way across the steep hillside. Carter grips the saddle horn tightly and I squeeze my arms around him. When we reach the top, I stop and let the horse blow, giving him a chance to catch his breath. Here you can see the Mission Mountains as they form a towering wall that runs from north to south. To the west, the lower Flathead River cuts a channel through sandy bluffs. And to the north, Flathead Lake forms a kind of inland ocean twenty-eight miles long, fifteen miles across, and hundreds of feet deep. Most of what I see lies within the boundaries of the Flathead Indian Reservation, the oldest reservation in Montana. Four tribes—the Salish, the Kootenai, the

Kalispel, and the Lower Pend d'Oreille—moved here after signing the Treaty of Hellgate in 1855. The treaty promised them protection from raiding Blackfeet Indians to the north. In 1910, parcels of land not allotted to tribal members were opened to homesteaders, and now non-Indian residents own just less than half of the land on the reservation.

Seen from above, the broad plain of the valley is checkerboarded with tiny farms and ranches. Little square pastures of cured grass covered in old snow, next to the black soil of freshly plowed fields. A red tractor bumps across a distant pasture, cattle strung out behind, feeding on last summer's hay.

I kiss the top of Carter's helmet, gently enough so that he doesn't feel it, and we ride down to the cattle grazing below.

The colt spends the short winter days penned in the muddy corral. He weighs seven hundred pounds now, and is fifteen months old. He shares the space with another horse, a lame gray mare that stands in one corner of the corral, waiting for the day the men will haul her to the sale ring in Kalispell.

Beneath the mud, the colt's coat is colored deep chocolate, turning light brown at the muzzle and darker on his legs. There is a coronet of white hair above his right rear hoof, and a small patch of white on his left wither that looks like a bird's been perched there. The black hair of his mane sticks up in a hundred different directions, but it is not quite long enough to become tangled. The colt's thin tail hangs like a sad flag. But in his own way, he is beautiful.

February. I saddle Draco, the stumblebum, while Phil grooms Dipper in the dim quiet of the barn. Our breaths—his and mine, the horses'—rise and collect in the cobwebs strung across the rafters. I slip the cold bit into Draco's mouth and buckle the cheekstrap of the bridle. I take the reins and lead him out of the barn and through the corrals, then stop to open the gate the cattle will come through. I tighten the cinch, then swing up into the saddle. Phil rides Dipper up one side of the triangular pasture and I take the other. We circle around the cows, pushing them down the hill to the corrals, calling out, "Let's go, girls."

I watch them as they move, looking for cows that are limping, searching for those with runny eyes or lumpy jaws. When I see an animal that needs attention, I take out my little spiral-bound notebook and a pen and jot down the cow's eartag number, a brief description of the animal, and the problem. ORANGE TAG # 258, RED BROCKLE, LEFT FRONT. Phil and I will treat the ailments when we run the cows through the squeeze chute back at the corral.

I love this work, the progression of the day ahead. The cows lined up in the alleyway, waiting to be preg-checked. The clang of the squeeze chute slamming closed. I know, at day's end, I will be blistered and beaten and maybe even bloodied, but I will sleep hard tonight. An old Hereford turns and faces me, wanting to know how serious I am about the process. "Get up there, you old hide," I say, and slap the ends of my reins on my leather chinks. She spins and trots to catch up with the other cows, and I follow, the last one off the hill.

At the corrals, I dismount and close the gate behind us. I tie Draco alongside Dipper in the barn, then gather the things we will need. Stainless steel vaccination guns with glass barrels. A box of fourteen-gauge needles, one and a half inches long. Blank eartags and a permanent marker. A bottle of antibiotic to treat pinkeye or lump jaw or hoof rot. Waterproof livestock markers, orange and red, like the crayons of giant children.

The horses paw the wooden floor of the barn. Outside, the cows mill around the corral. My boss looks at his watch and says, "I guess I should call." He walks off toward his house to see what is keeping the vet.

Phil does things differently than other ranchers in the area. His cows calve on green grass in May, instead of the usual March or April. Rather than working the herd in late fall, he waits until February. Bred cows get two vaccinations, one shot to prevent respiratory problems and another to guard against intestinal worms. Open cows, those that aren't bred, get big Xs drawn across their backs with a livestock crayon. They are culls which will be sorted off later, shipped to the auction yard in Missoula, and sold as beef.

Phil's ranch has a conservation easement placed on it, which means the four square miles of his property will never be subdivided. The ranch will always be open land. Phil protects the wildlife on his property as well, even animals that are considered varmints. Some of his neighbors begrudge him this indulgence because they think coyotes use his ranch as a safe place from which to roam. And Phil doesn't allow any chemicals on his land. Once, a neighboring farmer wanted to spray herbicide on a field they were working on shares, and Phil told him, "There's subtropical titmice in that field, Wayne." Later, he confessed to me, "I don't know where I came up with that titmouse bit, but it sounded good and it confused Wayne enough that he never sprayed the field." This place is a sanctuary, and I am grateful for it. It grounds me, and it fills my heart.

Phil walks back from the house carrying a battered green thermos and a stack of Styrofoam cups. "There was a message on my machine from Ray Rose saying he'll be able to lend a hand today. And I got in touch with the vet's office. Sounds like they got a new doctor and he went to Dublin Gulch instead of Valley View," he says. "Want some coffee?"

"Sure." I nod.

He pours us each a cup and we sit on the wooden catwalk above the alleyway leading to the squeeze chute. A red cow with a white face stares at us through the boards of the corral.

"What are cull cows worth these days?" I ask. When we were running the ranch in Miles City, I listened to the farm market reports every morning. I knew the price spread between an open cow and a bred one. I knew the cost of a ton of hay and a fifty-pound sack of horse feed. I'm not sure I ever really knew the true value of things, but I knew what they cost. Now, working as a hired hand, it's not so important anymore.

"You take what you get," Phil says. "It's never enough. Sometimes I think I'd be better off just selling the cows and leasing out the grass. I can't keep doing this forever. I have to think about the future."

The future. It slipped my mind for a moment. "I forgot to tell my news," I say. "Jennifer's expecting in late July. We're going to have twins."

"That'll keep you busy," he says, chuckling softly. He is the father of two girls and two boys.

We don't know yet if the babies are boys or girls or one of each. At the appointment I missed when I came out to the ranch with Carter, Jennifer's doctor confirmed the pregnancy, then ordered an ultrasound for the following week. "Either you're off on your conception date, or there's something else going on," she said. The ultrasound showed two fetuses. Baby A and Baby B. Two. Double everything. Most days, I'm able to handle this turn of events by shrugging and telling myself, "That's life. What are you going to do?" Other days I'm convinced we made a terrible mistake when we decided to have another child. We will need to get a bigger car. We'll have to remodel the house or move to another one with more bedrooms. I will never get around to buying a horse because there will already be too many mouths to feed.

But maybe I can work out a deal with Phil. Maybe I can keep the horse here and work extra hours in order to pay for its pasture. I take a breath, rehearse the words, and just as I am about to ask, Phil looks up and says, "There's Ray now."

A white pickup speeds down the county gravel, then

slows as it moves up the driveway, dodging potholes. The truck stops at the barn and a handful of men climb out. Ray Rose is in his midfifties. He manages a larger ranch that borders Phil's place. Ray has brought some of the Mexican guys he works with, Cowboy and Nestor and one other man I don't know. We're shaking hands and exchanging introductions when a tan pickup pulls down the driveway and parks alongside Ray's truck. The veterinarian steps out, already rolling up his sleeves. "They told me Dublin Gulch, not Valley View," he says. And it is time to get started.

Phil and Ray and the vet set up around the squeeze chute. The Mexicans and I use sorting sticks to move cows from the larger pen into the alleyway. The men speak only Spanish, but we don't need to talk. Everyone understands what needs to be done, and the cows know the routine. They move up from the large corral to the smaller pen in bunches, then crowd into the alleyway single file. Once a cow is in the squeeze chute, the vet moves quickly, palpating each one to determine if she is pregnant or not, calling out if she is "good" or "open." We work a hundred and fifty head in three hours and then break for lunch.

We sit on the front porch of Phil's two-story cedar house, slipping off our muddy boots. Cowboy says something in Spanish, pointing at an old coffee can on the porch. Phil laughs and says, *"Café, por jardin."* He turns to me and explains, "He thought I chewed a lot of Copenhagen to get a whole can full of tobacco, but those are coffee grounds. I'm saving them to fertilize the garden."

We enter the house through the utility room, padding

on the linoleum in our socks. There are stock prods, eartags, and big plastic calf bottles on the shelf above the washer and dryer. In the kitchen, the counter is loaded with sandwiches, bags of chips, napkins, and paper plates. "Help yourself to root beer and cream soda in the refrigerator," Phil says.

I load up a paper plate, grab a bottle of root beer, and sit on the couch in the living room. There are maps and posters thumbtacked to the walls. Across from me, there is a color illustration of Glacial Lake Missoula, the ancient body of water that shaped the land around us. The size of Lake Superior, it once covered three-thousand square miles and was two-thousand feet deep. Out the kitchen window, I can see ridges on the hills above the barn, the lap lines of the lake's high-water marks. I take a drink of root beer and think that, no matter how many fields we might plow, or how many holes we might dig in the ground, it is the land that shapes us.

After lunch, we finish the remaining one hundred cows. The vet and Ray and his crew head down the road. Phil and I sort the herd, turning the cull cows back to the corral and letting the rest out to pasture. "It was a good day," Phil says. "Thank you for your effort."

I get in my truck and drive down Apple Road for a mile, then turn east on the pavement of Eli Gap Road. I drive past a tiny pump house, two golden willows, and a trio of neglected McIntosh trees. Gone is the sad old house once sided with tar-paper shingles made to look like brick. The house had no foundation, its doors gaping like crooked teeth. The Rose place.

Jennifer and I almost lived here when we first came to the valley thirteen years ago. The local newspaper's classified ad listed the address and the rent, one hundred and eighty-five dollars a month. We drove out and saw the apple trees and the garden spot. Even then, the house was falling down before our eyes, but we didn't see it. To us, it was a perfect place to start life in the country. We phoned the landlord who told us the house had already been rented. I wonder what we would have become, had Jennifer and I moved into that old house on Eli Gap Road. Maybe we'd be in the same place we are today. Maybe our histories are already written.

A year ago, the Rose place burned down. Three of us met at our fire hall on the east shore of the lake on a Tuesday evening, then drove to the fire station in town. The fire chief went over the training exercise, drawing on the chalkboard where the engines should be parked, and after the briefing, the convoy of slow-moving fire trucks climbed the hill to the south. I wasn't sure where we were going, but when we turned onto Eli Gap Road, I had a feeling it was the Rose place. The trucks turned in to the yard and arranged themselves around the old house. Except for a mattress, some cardboard boxes, and a sprinkling of mouse droppings, the building was empty. Torch to cardboard to mattress. Flames rolled across the ceiling and banked down the walls. Windows popped, mice scurried outside, apples baked on the branches of the nearby trees. A plume of smoke boiled out of a broken window and drifted north. It was as if the place was ready to go. The firemen backed off to watch, the ashes of the Rose place peppering their yellow turnouts.

Now, as I drive past, all that remains is the smell of rotting apples, memory.

The red-haired man sorts the colt from the others in the large corral, then hazes the young horse into a small pen and latches the gate behind. He talks softly, saying, "Hey, Blackie," shaking a plastic bucket of oats. The brown colt noses the unsure air. Finally, he steps forward and nuzzles the grain out of the man's hand. It tastes of oats and summer, then, as he mouths the man's palm, motor oil and sweat. The man rubs his other hand along the colt's neck.

Each day, the man presses farther. Each day, the colt accepts a little more. First the man rubs the colt with his open hand, then with the blue nylon halter. He slips the halter over the colt's narrow nose and buckles it. The young horse steps away from the man, bobbing his head back and forth, up, then down. When he can't shake the halter, the colt stops and stands motionless, his head hanging.

The next day, the man snaps a ten-foot-long cotton lead rope to the halter. The colt walks around the corral, dragging the rope until it is caked in mud. Every so often, one of his hooves catches the rope, pulling him up short. By the end of the week, the colt has learned to give in to the tight rope, rather than resist it.

The man holds the crusty rope in one hand and strokes the horse's neck with the other. He clucks his tongue and walks around the corral, leading the young horse. After a half hour, he walks to the railroad tie set in the ground in the middle of the corral. He ties the rope to the solid post and steps away. The colt pulls back a little, testing the post. He waits. He paws the ground. He noses the railroad tie, smelling creosote and the blood of other, less gentle horses. And then he looks to the man, who smiles, his freckles scattering, and says, "You're too easy, Blackie."

In March, a snowstorm hits, pushing spring deeper into the year. The pages of the calendar turn and turn, time slips by unchecked. The expiration date on a jar of peanut butter catches me by surprise: *Best if sold by November.* By then, we will be through the pregnancy and the babies will be here.

An entirely new world, made of mirrors, welcomes us. Two babies was a possibility I hadn't considered. Twins don't run in either of our families and I don't even know any twins. They are something that happen to other people. They are a device used in made-for-television movies. Twins is one too many.

Another ultrasound shows they are boys. I secretly wanted a boy and a girl, so the two would be as different as possible. I'm anxious at the prospect of identical twins, worried we will name them Barry and Larry, dress them in matching outfits. "We'll have to join support groups for parents of multiples," I tell Jennifer. "And we can plan vacations to multiples conventions in the Twin Cities. It'll be great." Jennifer knows I'm joking. We are not joiners. If our boys are identical, we will do what we can to make them different. We don't even call them "the twins," preferring instead to call them "the babies" or "the boys."

We put all of our unspoken anxiety into fixing up our nest. Jennifer cleans out the closets. I build a bookcase along one wall of the family room. I try to organize the garage, but there is so much I am unwilling to throw away. All of the hobbies from the past, things I studied and pursued, only to leave them half-finished. Plastic buckets, a bottle capper, and five cases of empty bottles line one wall, relics of my attempts to brew beer. The macabre amateur taxidermy projects. Two drum sets I've been packing around since high school, stacked like tires in the corner.

Late one afternoon, just as I am about to head outside to shovel snow from the driveway, the phone rings. It's Tim, the man I worked for eight years ago. "I'm just going through St. Ignatius now," he says. "I was wondering if you had time to get a beer. I should be coming through town in forty-five minutes or so." We plan to meet near the highway, at the lounge in the bowling alley.

I agree to go out of habit, because I always used to say yes when Tim asked for anything. I worked on his ranch outside of Eureka, Montana, for three years. Since then, Tim and I have exchanged cards at Christmas, and occasional phone calls, but we haven't seen each other. I wonder if I'll recognize him, wonder if he still has a mustache and wears a gray felt cowboy hat, wonder if there will be a royal blue scarf knotted at his throat.

The snow turning to slush on the highway reminds me

of driving to Tim's ranch to doctor sick calves during spring storms. We'd shave the hair from the calf's neck and thread an IV into the vein, then drip a homemade solution of distilled water and glucose through the needle to rehydrate the animal. I remember the calves we saved, and the ones we lost. I remember the way Tim and I didn't need to talk to understand a thing: a mistake on my part, a harsh word on his, my fear of failure, his heartsickness over the departure of his girlfriend. Tim was more than a mentor to me, he was an older brother.

I pull into the parking lot of the bar alongside a big white Dodge pickup with a toolbox in the bed. The 56T prefix on the truck's license plates means it's from Lincoln County. It has to be Tim's. He used to drive Fords.

I push open the door to the lounge and walk around a bank of video poker and keno machines, their lights flashing to entice gamblers into betting their hearts and their hopes a nickel or a quarter at a time. Above the bar, a television is tuned to a college basketball game. Tim sits facing the television, a half-full glass of beer on the bar in front of him. I walk over, shake his hand, and take a seat on the next barstool. Eight years. An eyeblink, an eternity. It's hard to know where to begin.

The bartender is a twentysomething kid with fuzzy sideburns and a nervous smile. I order Tim another beer and one for myself. Instead of his cowboy hat, Tim wears a green baseball cap. He looks a little softer now, his hair gone silver, but—even in the artificial light of the television and neon beer signs—his eyes are the same pale blue of my memory, the color of a river. And I wonder how I look to him, eight years older, a father now, someone other than who I was when he was my boss, when he taught me that it is all right to want what you want, that you shouldn't make apologies for who you are or for who you want to be.

Tim points at his head and says, "This is me." And I think he is making a statement about who he is, a man sitting in a bar in a bowling alley in the middle of a Montana snowstorm. But Tim is pointing at the ball cap on his head, which advertises an excavating business. He now clears lots and constructs roads for people building new houses. We don't talk about the fact that when I left, Tim hauled his cows to town and sold them, then gave up his leased pastures. He bought heavy machinery—road graders and dump trucks and a low-boy trailer—things that might break down, but would never die like cattle, or quit him like I did.

Tim is married again, to a woman I've never met. "Jocelyn went out and bought two colts," he says. "I asked her, 'How are you gonna break them?' and she said, 'I'm not. You are.' So I've been working with them. They're gonna make nice horses," he says. "Pretty soon I'm going to saddle them up and see if they have any farts left in them."

Here is my chance to bring up the colt I want to buy. Maybe Tim will help me find a horse, help me train it. But I can't bring myself to ask. Too much time has passed, too many things have changed in both our lives. Instead, I say, "Jennifer and I are expecting twin boys at the end of July." He cocks an eyebrow, then raises his beer and we toast in silence.

The bartender refills our empty glasses. It's happy hour, cheap spirits and loose-jointed memories. Tim says, "I used to come down here when I was logging with horses in the North Fork." This was twenty-five years ago, when he first moved to Montana from Chicago. "There was this old boy who had a place right on the lake, just across from here." He tips his head to the north. "The San Francisco Ranch. He did all the work with Belgian draft horses. I used to come down and get help from him when a horse was giving me fits."

"What was his name?" I ask.

"Forrest Davis."

The name sounds familiar to me, and I turn it over in my mind. Then I remember I've seen it painted on the side of a restored horse-drawn wagon that sits in the parking lot of Three Dog Down, the down-comforter outlet. FORREST DAVIS FREIGHT COMPANY.

"I think he's still around," I say.

Tim shakes his head. "There's no way. He was old when I knew him. If he's alive, he's got to be a hundred by now."

I shrug and drink my beer.

"How old are you?" Tim asks.

"Thirty-six."

"I'd give anything to be in my thirties again," he says. "You still ranching?"

"Working for a guy part-time." I haven't been out to the ranch since we preg-checked the cows. It's been three weeks. And I miss it, the work and the horses. I miss being cold and tired and coming home to a warm house. "It's not a lot of hours, just enough to keep me honest." It is getting late, and Tim still has a hundred and a half miles to drive in the dark.

Outside, the snow is still falling. I say, "It's been too long."

"Yeah, it has," Tim says. "You'll have to drive up some day. Bring your family along to meet Jocelyn."

A flood of lights from the Wal-Mart and Safeway stores brightens the sky to the south of us. A new car wash and medical clinic are to the east. There is a savings and loan to the west. But even through the snow, you can see that this was once just a cow pasture. Old fence posts line one end of the parking lot. Across the highway, there is a golf-course housing development, executive homes built along the lakeshore. The excavators and bulldozers are parked for the night. Strings of tiny flags flap in front of the model homes like flocks of waterfowl. Adjacent to this development, there is another, even more exclusive subdivision planned. A custom ironwork gate hangs at the front entrance, the metal cut into silhouettes of cattails and ducks, and it bears the name of the place: Mission Preserve. Executive homes in a small Montana town with no industry other than tourism and cattle and timber. This is where the San Francisco Ranch used to be, where Forrest Davis worked his big Belgians and where Tim came to learn about horses. In a distant corner of the field, there is a huge wooden contraption, called a beaver slide, once operated by draft horses to stack loose hay. It is a weathered gray skeleton now, a relic, and I wonder if it has been left for décor, or if the developers simply haven't had time to tear it down yet. And I wonder if Forrest Davis is really still alive, the man who mentored my mentor.

The colt stands dozing in the small corral. His rump rests against the railroad tie in the middle of the pen. His head droops and his ears hang limply. One leg is cocked and he dreams horse dreams. The colt's head picks up at the sound of the gate latch. The red-haired man is there, holding the lead rope. He pets the colt on the neck, whispering, "Sorry about this, Blackie, but we got to do it before fly season."

The other man stands at the rails of the corral, sharpening a small knife. The blade flashes in the April sun, reflecting clouds and mountains. "Tie him up and get enough Ace to dope him good," the man says. "That last one fought like a drunk monkey."

The red-haired man ties the rope to the railroad tie. He will have to unfasten it later, when his father injects the colt with the tranquilizer and the horse goes down. Then he'll unsnap the rope from the halter and tie it around one of the colt's rear hocks, so he can lift the leg and expose the horse's testicles.

He opens the gate and heads to the house for the sedative, his father calling out, "And don't forget the iodine."

Each day pulses with wild joy. I finish building the bookcase. Jennifer sorts through baby clothes and washes them. A friend loans us a second crib to go with the one we have stored in the garage. We will set them up in our bedroom.

On the refrigerator door, Jennifer tapes the cover from

a glossy parenting magazine, a photograph of twin boys, white-blond hair, perfect teeth, running hand in hand across a beach. The picture shows us who our boys might be. It helps us imagine the future. Meanwhile, Jennifer gets bigger and bigger, carrying her weight out in front of her. There are three months left and I don't know how she'll make it.

The phone rings and it's Phil, my boss. I am happy to hear his voice, ready to say yes, to come out to the ranch when he asks. He says, "I just wanted to make sure that we are square on your hours."

"Yes," I say. "We're good."

"Well that's just right then." He pauses and I think, for a moment, that we've been disconnected. "I sold the cows," he says finally. "I'll be leasing the grass out to Hughes."

I can't think of a thing to say. I don't know whether to congratulate him or offer my sympathy. "I'll come out and get my gear sometime," I say. "I'll call first."

Jennifer looks up from the crib she is assembling in our bedroom. "Who was that?" she asks.

How quickly things can change, yet how slowly. It is the same feeling I had twelve years ago when I was let go from Calvin Brown's ranch after he sold his land to the Tribe. It is a loss. I hoped I would be training a colt in the corrals at Phil's ranch, riding those hills with Carter and his little brothers for years to come. I can't remember all I have left there. Saddle, blanket, pad, reins and halter, chinks, maybe a jacket. Those things are easily found. What can't be reclaimed is the hole in my story, the empty space on that line that used to read "cowboy" or "ranch hand" or "man with horse." I need a new story.

It's a week later when I find one, though it is not my own. It is a tale of the Old West, a time when longhorn cattle flowed north from Texas like a rust-colored river. I hold a book in my hand, *We Pointed Them North: Recollections of a Cowpuncher*. The story of Teddy Blue Abbott, as told to Helena Huntington Smith, just before he died. I page through the book and see the words "broomtail" and "bellyful." I see "Miles City" and "Musselshell" and "Powder River." All familiar to me, names and places from the past.

Like an old photograph, Abbott's story is told in black-and-white. As I read it, my memory colors the pages, remembering how the broken landscape goes on and on to the horizon. The arid rangeland outside Miles City, Montana, where Abbott spent his cowboy wages on women and whiskey, is the same place I tried to hold together a ranch. The past is prologue.

What I remember most about moving away from southeast Montana and coming back to the mountains was how rampant life seemed here, how the trees and the brush are rabid, how the wilderness grows right to the edge of the road and leans over. Life, out of control.

Four in the morning. My head spins, the light from the bathroom wheeling in and out. I'm adrift, floundering, and Jennifer is saying, "My water just broke." It's much too early on all accounts: the hour, the day, the month. It's still seven weeks till her due date. And now Jennifer is clutching a pale yellow bath towel between her legs. "Should I call the doctor? Should we go to the hospital? Should we wake up Carter?" I am trying to piece it all together. My jeans. Carter. The phone. Christ, she has a lot of fluid coming out of her. Jennifer calls the emergency room at the hospital in town. They tell her to come in as soon as she can. I dress Carter in the first clothes I find: sweatpants, a raincoat over his pajama tops, mismatched socks. Jennifer waddles out to the car. We drive to town in the dark, deer darting away from the headlights of our car.

At the hospital, after a quick check by the on-call physician, a nurse tells us, "They're going to ship you down to Missoula," sixty-five miles south, to the nearest hospital with a neonatal intensive care unit. I lean over and steal a quick kiss from Jennifer, telling her everything is going to be all right. She nods and says, "I know," but her eyes tell me she isn't buying any of it. There is no more time. The ambulance is waiting.

The nurse told me the doctors will most likely delay delivery for a day, maybe two. I buckle Carter into his car seat and we drive back home to pack. I grab a pillow, gather some coloring books and toys for Carter, then head out again.

We drive south on Highway 93, the narrow two-lane road that will take us to Missoula. It is a sunny day in the first week of June, and the drive is a blur of bright green fields and blue gray mountains, glaciers white on the face of McDonald Peak. Beautiful Sunday. I think of Jennifer riding down to the hospital in the windowless compartment of the ambulance. The contractions, the worry, seven weeks before her due date. She is unable to see any of the passing beauty.

I remind myself that twins are fairly common. Two babies are nothing new. And this other stuff happens all the time as well—ambulances, IVs, medicine to delay contractions. But they don't happen to us.

When we get there, the hospital parking lot is mostly empty. A bored security guard stands in the shade of the awning at the entrance. He squints at me and nods. It's 10 a.m. Carter and I walk through the revolving door, down the hallway, to the "Mother & Baby Unit." At the front desk, a blonde nurse wearing maroon scrubs smiles and says, "I know who you are. Let me get someone to watch your little guy and you can meet your new sons." I open my mouth, but nothing comes out. She adds quickly, "Don't worry, everybody's fine."

The boys have arrived, earlier and earlier, everything rushing forward faster, faster, faster. The nurse takes us to an empty hospital room and she turns the television to cartoons. She gets Carter a twin orange Popsicle and a paper cup to catch the drips. "I'll take you to the NICU then come back and sit with him," the nurse offers. I kiss Carter on the head and tell him that I am going to go see Mommy and his brothers and that I will be right back.

The nurse leads me down the hallway to the locked door of the NICU. The "nick-you," the one place Jennifer never wanted to be. She enters a code into the keypad outside the locked door and I follow her instructions. At the sink, I wash my hands, soaping and scrubbing them for three long minutes. I take off my ball cap, but don't know where to put it, so I drop it in the corner, out of the way. Then I don a flimsy hospital gown, white with pale blue stripes. The nurse says, "They're around the corner, to the right. I'll go back and sit with your other one."

"Thanks," I say, then turn to meet my new sons. Each of the babies lies in a clear plastic box, his own isolette. And though I tried to prepare myself for how small they would be, I had no idea what four-and-a-half pounds really meant. Wires connect monitors to tiny feet, hands, hearts. IVs and stomach tubes. Two little boys pulled into a big, big world. When Carter was born, Jennifer was admitted at ten at night and she gave birth at three the next afternoon. I held her hand the entire time. This time, I missed it all.

Jennifer is wheeled into the room on a bed, her hair all crazy, her nose bright red, scratched raw. "You made it," she says, her voice soft and gravelly. She itches her nose, a reaction to the anesthesia. "Sorry we had to start without you." She manages a smile. She is so beautiful.

"You did good," I say. I know that it doesn't really matter how we got here, early or late. Everything is going to work out. Everything will be fine, once the world slows down a little.

Jennifer is wheeled back to the recovery room, where Carter is waiting for her. I stand and stare at the tiny pink dolls in the clear plastic boxes. I watch the solution dripping from the bag to the IV tube, and each drip is another dollar gone. We have a little money saved, but I have no job. Drip, drip. Everything times two. I want to rip off my hospital gown and put my dusty cap back on. I want my hands to be dirty, to be out of this stale sour air.

Instead, I untie my hospital gown and drop it into the laundry basket by the door. I grab my cap and walk back to the recovery room.

I phone grandparents and deliver the news. Carter watches cartoons. Jennifer nods off. Time disappears. In the tiny kitchen across the hall from Jennifer's room, I raid the refrigerator for little packs of chocolate pudding, cups of ice chips, half-sized cans of lemon-lime soda and ginger ale. Just before dinner, I scrub my hands and put on another gown and visit the boys again. Someone has taped a card over each isolette, one reading AVERY, the other BENNETT. This is me, I think. This is my life.

☆　☆　☆

The boy doesn't remember any of this: he was born in Cranwich Hall, in the town of Cranwich, in the eastern part of England, in the county of Norfolk, a week before Christmas, on December 17, 1860. His mother, Ann, and father, James, name their son after his paternal grandfather, Edward. They call him Teddy for short.

He remembers the sickness, though. He was born small. Big eyes, frail frame, the hollow weight of a barn cat. He is prone to spells of weakness and chills. Just before his family packed up and left Cranwich, the family doctor told his mother to keep him outdoors as much as possible. It was the only cure.

The boy, along with his mother and father and the other children, Jimmy, Frank, Harry, Ann, Gertrude, and Ruth, board the ship in Liverpool. Eleven days later, on June 28, 1871, the ship docks in Quebec. From there, the family heads south, to Nebraska. They arrive in Lincoln, which is as far as the train can take them. Beyond is nothing but land. It is a gorgeous June day, occasional clouds pearling the blue distance. The world is a wide-open place.

Three thousand people call Lincoln home. Coyotes roam the muddy streets. Antelope race the edges of the city. The family rents a house in town while James looks for a homestead. He finds a quarter-section of bottomland located twelve miles southwest of Lincoln, on the Haines Branch of Salt Creek. He pays the Burlington & Missouri River Railroad Company twenty-four hundred dollars for a hundred and sixty acres. There are only six other settlers in the area. This arid place is so far from Cranwich, where they could smell the North Sea. The family does its best to inhabit this unfamiliar land.

I buckle Carter into his car seat and we drive south, through Pablo, then on through the small farming community of Ronan. To the east, the foothills and rounded peaks of the Missions give way, turning jagged and foreboding. Twelve thousand years ago, a huge glacier crept south from northern Canada. Thousands of feet thick and hundreds of miles wide, the glacier stopped its advance here, where the land is now potholed with tiny ponds. Each watery hole was once a chunk of ice, pushed along with sand and gravel ahead of the advancing glacier. When the glacier retreated and the great chunks of ice melted, they became ponds, home to ducks and geese, blue herons and trumpeter swans.

On the west side of the highway, I catch sight of a greasy stain on the pavement. It leads to a carcass in the grassy ditch. A bear. We are past before I can tell if it's a grizzly or a black bear.

Onward, past the oldest building in Montana, a tiny log cabin that was once part of Fort Connah, established in 1846 as a trading post for trappers. Past the town of St. Ignatius, with its historic brick Catholic church, the namesake of the Mission Mountains. Past the National Bison Range, a refuge established in 1908 to protect the last of the great buffalo herds that once roamed the plains. The Bison Range is eighteen thousand five hundred fenced acres of grass, home to three hundred bison. Down the steep hill into Ravalli, where another black bear stands on the railroad tracks that parallel the highway. The animal moves like a puppet, standing on its hind legs as if on invisible strings. It noses the air, head high, looking across the highway, weighing its options. "Look, Carter, a bear," I say, but it is already gone.

We drive down Evaro Hill and across the Interstate, into Missoula, which Carter calls "Busytown." We drive past the airport and the Smokejumper Center with the Forest Service tankers—old Air Force bombers—parked on the runway, waiting for fire season. Onto Reserve Street, where all of the big box stores have sprung up, one after another. Appliances and building materials and discount clothes and sporting goods. Fast-food restaurants, convenience stores. Carter stares.

In the hospital parking lot, two men are racing electric wheelchairs across the pavement, bumping over curbs and potholes. Carter and I watch them laugh and taunt each other as they spin around the lot. "Let's go find Mommy," I say. It's Wednesday and Jennifer is coming home.

She is dressed and ready to go when we get to her room, yet she lingers. We will be leaving without our babies. They are still in the NICU, sleeping constantly. The monitors blink and beep. The IVs drip. The boys get two cc's of milk through a stomach tube at each feeding. It is nothing, just a few drops, but it's all they can handle. We will rent a breast pump from the hospital, and one of us will drive down every day with Jennifer's milk. "It'll be three weeks, maybe four," the pediatrician tells us. She is a confident doctor, reassuring, with short strawberry blond hair and a warm smile. "While they're here, I'd like to do some tests on Avery," she adds, explaining that there is a particular crease in his palm that she is concerned about, and that his ears seem to be set a little low on his face. I shrug my shoulders. Jennifer nods. After all we've been through, what's one more test? It is Bennett I am worried about. He is still on oxygen and he is two ounces lighter than his brother.

Carter and I stand in the hallway outside the NICU and look through the window. Jennifer is saying good-bye to the babies. She lifts the lid of Avery's isolette and picks him up through the tangle of wires and tubes. She kisses him on top of his purple-and-white knit cap, then returns him to the box and does the same with Bennett. Behind Carter and me, on the wall across from the window, there is a gold-and-silver tree. On each golden leaf there is the name of a baby who was born in the hospital. Each silver leaf is engraved with the name of a baby who never made it home.

I need to move, need to breathe. Carter and I walk to the snack shop, a small room with vending machines and a few tables. Carter looks over his options and decides on a bag of cookies. They are frosted in pink and white, decorated with colorful sprinkles. Each cookie is in the shape of a circus animal. Lions and tigers. I think of the dead bear I saw earlier, and the live one standing on the railroad tracks. Everything suddenly seems so fragile, so breakable, so lost.

The boy needs help getting on and off his horse. His legs fall short of the stirrups. His father wants to tie him to the saddle in case he gets washed into the current of the Red River, but—even at the age of ten—Teddy knows this is a bad idea. Fresh graves line the banks of the Red, resting places of unfortunate cowboys who didn't make it across the treacherous water. Teddy argues with his father, telling him he's a good swimmer and that he doesn't want to go down with the horse if it quits him. They watch the river as a large tree limb rushes past. A cowboy, the one with the cloudy eye, nods to Teddy's father who purses his thin lips and says, "Have it your way, boy."

Three hundred longhorn steers wait to ford the Red and follow the trail north to Nebraska. The water runs crimson from the sediment of the red bluffs lining the banks, but to the boy it looks like a river of blood. They put the loose horses in first, hoping the cattle will follow. "They start milling and we're all in," the cloudy-eyed cowboy shouts. The men crowd the cattle from behind, pushing the lead steers into the water. Teddy clings to his horse's neck and squeezes his legs as tight as he can, spurring the horse forward. He is too afraid to let go long enough to whip his reins across the horse's rump. When the horse's feet leave the bottom, it feels like they are soaring. The herd finally emerges on the other side of the river, a half mile downstream from where it went in.

Once across, they are in that territory known as the Indian Nations. The cowboys take a head count. Only one little steer was lost when it turned back, then got swept under. Teddy's father shouldn't have bought the steer in the first place; it was too weak to make the trip. Now, the old man nods to the boy, turns his horse, and rides to the nearest stage stop. He leaves the rest of the work to the hired men, to his ten-year-old son. He'll take the stage back to New Orleans, then board the train bound for Lincoln.

Teddy keeps his mouth shut and his eyes open, trying to learn as much as he can. One of the cowboys is missing three fingers on his right hand. Another takes his hat off and shows the boy where a Union bullet creased his skull, the War Between the States just a few years cold. While the men were away fighting, herds of longhorns multiplied and grew wild on the Texas plains. And now there is demand for cattle in the north.

They follow the Texas trail, beaten into the ground by six hundred thousand head of cattle taken off the range that year alone. Teddy helps with the horses as best he can, gathering them in the gray dawn light. The cowboys each use three or four horses a day, and the herd covers an average of fifteen miles. Each night, before they are turned out, Teddy tends to the horses' raw withers, reaching as high as he can to slather them with ointment when he has it, mud when he doesn't. He is a small boy, and there is not much more he can do.

In a week, his back is sore from sleeping on the hard ground. He is tired of cactus needles and rattlesnakes and bad water. The cook tells the men the bacon is just about gone. "It's beef from here on out." They have covered less than one hundred miles in the last week, and home is still five hundred miles north.

My mother and father drive six hundred miles north from their home in Wyoming to help however they can.

Friday, June 13. My mother has driven Jennifer down to the hospital to drop off the day's milk and visit the babies. Carter and my father play in Carter's room. I read Teddy Blue's story, escaping into his world, if only for a while.

When my mom and Jennifer return from the hospital, Jennifer passes straight through the house to our bedroom. I ask my mother, "Is everything all right?"

Her eyes betray her. "The boys have gained weight," she says.

Jennifer comes back into the living room, takes my hand, and leads me down the hallway. She closes the bedroom door and we sit on the bed and she leans into me and starts crying. And then she tells me.

Since the morning Jennifer's water broke, just five days

ago, everything has been moving forward faster and faster, an impossible acceleration of time. But now, it all stops. Doors slam shut between the passing seconds. Avery is not the son we thought we'd have. The family we once imagined is gone. I notice a new pattern on the comforter cover. Where I once saw the tiny triangles of Santa Claus hats, I now see its inversion, which looks like hundreds of birds flying south. I notice the fineness of the light through the window. I can hear our neighbor's dogs barking.

Jennifer and I hold each other and we cry. We grieve for Avery, for his future. Or maybe our sadness is for ourselves, for the loss of who we thought we were. We thought it didn't matter, this notion of perfect children. At less than a week old, Avery has been labeled, limited, his life foreclosed on, his future told by a crease in his tiny palm.

My father, just a wall away, is constructing an out-of-control Lego development with Carter. He needs to be told. But all I want to do is crawl under the comforter and vanish. I want to find a hole and climb into it and disappear.

I want this all to go away.

Teddy stands at the edge of his brother's grave, the rest of the family gathered behind. It is cold, the children bundled against the bottomless grief. The only one who doesn't feel the chill is the oldest, Jimmy.

Teddy stands, skinny and shivering, next to his older brother Harry. Young boys, two years apart in age, who are tied together by blood and work. The last dead person Teddy saw, Harry was there too. It was winter and they were feeding cows. Harry was up in the loft pitching loose hay down onto the loop of rope on the ground. Teddy pulled it out the barn door and fed the hay to the slatted, hollow-eyed cattle. It took forever. Like the scream dying in Harry's throat. Teddy climbed the ladder to the loft and saw what Harry had sunk his pitchfork into. A crazy woman from the asylum at the head of Haines Branch outside of Lincoln. She had stuck to the brushy draw of the creek, like a scared animal, following the drainage south and west, eight or nine miles, until she found their barn, the haystack, sleep, and the killing cold. Just a girl, waxy and blue as February. She wore a nightgown and nothing else. Teddy ran to the house as fast as he could, falling twice. Later, he and Harry had to return to the barn and finish feeding the cattle.

That first winter was a sort of death for all of them. The snow and the cold blowing in without mercy. Of the three hundred thin-skinned Texas steers his father had started with, only one hundred survived.

Teddy stands at the edge of the grave, remembering the dead girl in the haystack, remembering Jimmy. He was nothing like her, not in life, at least. Nineteen. Strong as a team of mules. The doctor came too late. By then, it sounded as if he were drowning from within. Teddy loved Jimmy the best, more than Harry or his mother, certainly more than his father. He asked his mother if God could have done something to keep Jimmy from dying, and she nodded and explained that God had the power to do anything he wanted. And Teddy cursed her God, shouted that he would never go to church again, would never worship a god that could take his brother like that.

Teddy concentrates on his feet, willing the blood into the ends of toes, which are forced into the too small boots he wears. The boots are a year old, but like new, since he is always in the saddle. People don't see that he is growing up. The next time he and Harry build a warming fire while feeding cows, Teddy will hold his feet too close to the flames, will char the soles of the boots in order to get a new pair. And when his mother takes him to town, Teddy will make sure he gets a pair large enough to last him. He is thinking all this through, concentrating on his toes so much, that he doesn't feel the wind playing around his head. It lifts his hat into the air like a black felt bird, a wing-shot raven, tumbling through the sky, into the open grave. His father, watery gray eyes fixed on the horizon, doesn't notice. His mother nods toward the grave. Teddy hangs over the lip of the open mouth of the ground that swallowed Jimmy and he retrieves his hat. It feels good to be off his feet. Reaching down into the unforgiving ground, he wonders if it hurts to be dead. Because, even at eleven years old, Teddy knows that, sometimes, it hurts like hell to be alive.

Chapter Two

HE STANDS ALONE IN A PASTURE
BUT NOBODY CAN SEE HIM.

HE HAS BEEN MADE INVISIBLE
BY HIS OWN WOUNDS.

I KNOW HOW HE FEELS.
> —RICHARD BRAUTIGAN,
> "War Horse"

Picture the colt. He's two years old now, and he weighs nine hundred pounds. His dark brown coat, shaggy with winter, gathers the fading Montana light. A dozen white hairs form the faintest of stars on his forehead. Snow falls, the flakes gathering on his back. He stands, completely motionless except for the flicker of an ear, the rise and fall of his ribs, the pulse of his heart.

A large buckskin gelding moves in close to the brown colt, ears pinned back, head down. The colt looks away. The buckskin stretches his neck and pretends to bite the young brown horse. The colt tucks his tail, but it is not enough for the buckskin. He bites down on the little white patch of hair on the colt's withers.

A cold wind blows in off the December lake. Tiny stars of light along the tops of houses near the highway, flashing, flashing. It is late in the day when the men finally come to feed. They smell of brandy and cigar smoke and new leather gloves. They feed the horses an extra bucket of oats and there is another bale of hay. It is Christmas Day, and the blessings are small and pure.

After they've eaten, the buckskin and the brown colt face each other and groom each other, mouthing neck and mane and shoulders, as the snow collects on their backs.

☆ ☆ ☆

The cowboy wears a black felt Stetson, a yellow plaid shirt, pointy-toed leather boots flecked with manure, and a black insulated jacket with bits of green hay flakes clinging to the sleeves. He's got a strawberry blond mustache, and a big smile. The man looks up from the envelopes in his hands and asks, "What do you know?"

"Not much, Bob," I say. "How about you?"

A chance meeting in the post office, along a wall of keyed boxes. I've come to pick up packages, birthday presents for Carter that are too big to fit in our mailbox. And here is Bob Ricketts, the owner of Three Dog Down, getting his mail. I've spoken with Bob a few times since hearing him sing at the bar that night, more than a year ago, with my father-in-law. I exchanged small talk with him in the hardware store last summer, when we were both buying plastic gas cans. Then again, just two weeks ago, I talked with Bob in his store, when I was buying Jennifer a comforter cover for Christmas.

He smiles and asks, "How's the family?"

Even though I've had enough practice in the last seven months, I don't know what to say. The truth wasn't always the right answer. After the emergency C-section, Avery was diagnosed with Down syndrome, and then Bennett had some problems of his own. Early on, Jennifer and I had difficulty knowing what to tell people when they asked with bright smiles, "How are the babies?" We tried out different versions of the story.

Bennett is finally doing all right, but Avery's been diagnosed with Down syndrome.

Have you ever heard of Down syndrome?

Avery has Down syndrome.

The responses were awkward, at best. More often than not, the smiles dimmed and there was a moment of silence, followed by something along the lines of, "Oh, but Down's kids are so happy and loving."

And I've become the defensive parent, the raw nerve. I want to answer, "You don't know my son." I try to remind myself that a year ago, if the situation were reversed, I would have responded, "But besides the Down syndrome, he's healthy, right?"

I finally worked out a way to answer the question *How are the babies?* If the person I'm talking with is someone I know only in passing, I don't mention Avery's condition. I just say that after the rough start of the babies arriving early, everything is going well. But if the person is someone I know, I explain as best I can, trying to sound optimistic, hoping for the best.

"Carter's doing great," I tell Bob, "and the little guys are coming along. I don't know if I told you or not, but Avery was diagnosed with Down syndrome."

"Yeah," Bob says. "I know. How is he doing?"

"Well, he's behind Bennett in terms of getting things figured out, but he has a sweet disposition and that goes a long way."

"Yes, it does," Bob says. "Say, I don't know what your situation is, but I have work for you if you need it. I have a lot of old fence that needs taken down, weeds that need spraying. Can you operate a bulldozer?"

I hold my hands out and pretend like I'm operating a bulldozer, but I feel like a fool, so I lower my arms and shrug.

"Well, you're going to learn. And I've got four of those Oberlander colts that need riding. You know how to drive, don't you?"

"Yeah," I laugh. "I've been driving since I was sixteen."

"No," Bob says. "I mean drive horses, like steer a team of horses."

"Oh no, I don't know anything about that. I really don't know much about training horses either," I admit. Here is my chance to tell someone about my plan to buy a horse of my own. And so, before I think too much about it, I just say the words. "I've actually been thinking about finding a colt and training it this summer."

"Do it at my place," Bob says. "I'll show you where

everything is and you can come and go as you please. My round pen is a little big, but it'll do. And I'm going to put sand in it this year. About the fourth or fifth time I got bucked off last summer, I was laying there on the hard ground, and I looked over and saw my tractor, and it finally hit me that I could work up the ground a little, make it softer."

A job and a place to train a colt. This is such a gift, out of the blue on a cold, gray day. Ever since I became a father—and especially in the last year, with Avery and Bennett—I feel as if I've been disappearing, losing parts of myself the way blood leaves the extremities of an animal when it begins to freeze. Tails and ears and feet going numb and dying, the cold working its way toward the heart. Time and energy and money, all going by the board. Right now, I feel a glimmer of hope that things might go back to how they once were. Maybe I can get a colt and remember what it is I love about being out in the West. The pieces of my life will fall into place again and everything will make sense.

"I'll trade you work for board," I say. "I'll take up that old fence and do whatever you need done. I'll clean stalls. You name it."

"I usually don't keep anything in a stall unless it's sick."

"I'll clean your house then," I say, laughing.

He turns serious. "Let me tell you something. When I was going through my divorce, I just checked out for about six months. I didn't do anything. Then I decided to hire a cleaning woman to tidy up the place a little. She walked in, took a look around, and left Montana without a word. Seriously, she left the state."

I laugh, shaking my head in disbelief. I haven't heard my own laugh in a long time, and it echoes in the lobby of the post office.

"Wait for this snow to melt," Bob says, "then give me a call."

Teddy wakes in the morning, cold and hungry. He builds a small campfire, struggling to get a rotten cottonwood branch to catch. Stale bread and a piece of cheese for breakfast. The same for lunch. He saddles Pete in the dark and mounts up at dawn. The boy rides out into the spring day, the sun just lightening the horizon.

He is glad to be away from the homeplace. His father gets worse with each passing day. The man is hard on all of his boys, but especially on big-eyed Teddy. Lincoln, Nebraska, America, has turned him into a shell, the constant wind and work wearing away at him. He sits in his room and runs callused fingers through his long white whiskers. He went to Cambridge, but nothing ever came of it. His brothers, Teddy's uncles, are solicitors back in London. They send their brother newspapers which he reads again and again, though they are weeks out-of-date. He wonders what he should have done differently. He is a man, alone.

Not long after they moved to America, Teddy's grandfather died back in Cranwich, and Teddy's father inherited ten thousand dollars. He sank the money into improvements, trying to make the place like an English estate—poplar trees planted around the house, benches for sitting, a pond stocked with German carp. The money kept the ranch afloat for a while, but the place is a leaky boat in a sea of grass.

The land changes before their eyes. Each train into Nebraska brings another load of hopefuls, another carload of dreams. The Texas trail brings cattle north to the railhead at Lincoln, so that anybody can stake out a homestead and start a ranch. His father was smart to have settled on the place on Haines Branch. The broken country above the ranch is uninhabitable. It is good cheap grazing for the longhorns. North of Lincoln, there is nothing but nothing. Wilderness. Indians.

Teddy's horse picks its way across the ridge. The boy looks down to the bottomland and remembers when the Pawnee came through, traveling from the reservation on the Loup River north of Lincoln down to the Republican River for their annual buffalo hunt. It was spring. Hundreds of men and women and children—their belongings packed onto their horses and the fast, fearless buffalo ponies saved for the hunt trailing behind—made camp near his father's place. Most of the Indians spoke broken English, and Teddy raced his pony against the young boys and their horses, imagining he was one of them.

When the Pawnee took down their camp and headed south across the country, Teddy went home and got his old shotgun and some blankets. He saddled Pete and left in the night, riding fifteen miles to finally catch up to the Pawnee in the morning. The chief of the tribe told him to go home.

The old man already had enough trouble in his life, and didn't need anyone thinking he'd kidnapped a twelve-year-old white boy. Teddy obeyed. Two months later, the hunting party returned, their horses loaded down with enough buffalo meat to see the band of Indians through the winter. That was the last Teddy saw of them. When his father found out about it, Teddy caught hell for running away. But his mother intervened.

She's a stern-looking woman. Her dark hair is parted severely in the middle, and there is an old woman's pull around her mouth, but she is kind. She has the same huge searching eyes that Teddy has. Back in Norfolk, she was raised with maids and housekeepers, music lessons and rose gardens. Here, in Nebraska, she tries to make ends meet, tries to sort flour from dust. She's had thirteen children over the years, but some were lost along the way. She worries about Teddy the most, worries that he will be lost too.

Carter unwraps the gift. It's a dozen two-inch-tall plastic figures. A red cowboy holds a six-shooter in each hand, his legs bowed, his boots molded into the small oval base. He stands his ground. A tan Indian holds a long spear. Two feathers stick upright from his head like bunny ears, and he holds a shield decorated with more feathers. His legs are spread, to straddle one of the two brick-red horses that are frozen midgallop. The other cowboys aim rifles, the Indians shoot bows and arrows. The set comes with a two-foot-square vinyl landscape to spread on the floor. It's printed with pine trees and mountains and a running river for the plastic Indian canoe. Fiery explosions are printed onto the background, flashes of gunfire rising out of the ground.

Carter lays out the pieces on the little patch of landscape. He has the cowboys make coffee over a campfire; they invite the Indians to share it with them. The plastic teepee, in Carter's eyes, is an outhouse for everyone to use. The cowboys and the Indians race their horses. They canoe together. Carter calls the explosions on the vinyl background "hot lava pits." There is no shooting or fighting or war. It looks like a wonderful place to live.

I think back to the time, a year ago, when Carter and I were riding on the ranch, a time that now seems so beautifully simple. Jennifer was pregnant. I had work, real work. It didn't pay much, but I slept well after coming home from a day on the ranch. I remember the view from the top of the hill, everything laid out below, the cowboys, the Indians, the patchwork of winter fields. Now it all seems like a distant child's game, only the rules don't quite make sense to me anymore. After the shock of the twins and the emergency C-section and Avery's diagnosis, I've lost all confidence that I can dream up plans and make them come true.

A black SUV pulls down the gravel drive and stops. The horses gather in front of the wire gate, waiting to be fed. A short man gets out of the passenger's side, his leather dress shoes sinking into the muddy ground. He scowls and pushes his eyeglasses up on the bridge of his nose, then reaches into the backseat for his rubber overshoes, which he pulls on one at a time. The man wears a clean canvas barn jacket over his white dress shirt. He struggles to open the wire gate. The driver rolls his window down and says, "Try the other side." The short man slogs over and loosens the wire. He waves his free hand at the horses gathered there, nervous that they will run him over. He looks to the driver for help. "Open it and get out of the way," the driver says before gunning the vehicle through the gap.

When the gate is closed again, the men drive to the far north end of the pasture, where the grass turns to cattails and reeds. The driver cuts the engine and gets out of the truck. He wears jeans and insulated boots, and has a black ball cap on his head. He towers over the shorter man. They walk around the horse pasture, each holding a piece of paper. The horses nose the air, smelling the cedar and sage of cologne from one of the men, cigarette smoke, and coffee. The smaller man points at the fence line, the driver gestures toward the lake. The grass has been grazed down to nothing, but the men still can't find the survey marker they are looking for. The shorter man searches through weeds, the taller man kicks open piles of manure. Finally the taller man finds the marker, stuck in the ground like a huge brass pushpin, marking the corner of the lot. The horses can hear the bigger man better, because his voice is low and quiet. The other man's voice is carried away on the wind. The men walk along the banks of the small creek that flows through the pasture. It is just a trickle of water, enough for the horses to drink from. The smaller man takes a camera from the pocket of his barn jacket and snaps a few photographs. The two men pace off the property and make notes on their papers. They take one last look at the skinny horses, then leave the way they came.

It is three-thirty in the morning and I am up with Bennett. The babies aren't on the same schedule and one always needs something. I thought twins would be easier. I imagined two fresh diapers, two bottles, and it's off to sleep. But the work has more than doubled. It's tripled, quadrupled maybe. I've changed more diapers and fed more bottles and been more of a parent in the last nine months than I ever was with Carter, and my contributions are only a fraction of the work Jennifer does. It is simply overwhelming, and there is no end in sight.

I lie on the sofa with Bennett in the crook of my arm. I feel trapped by his tiny weight. Pinned down. I should have called about the horse I saw advertised in the local newspaper yesterday. THREE-YEAR-OLD GELDING. GREEN BROKE. GENTLE. $800, WILL DELIVER. I should have called, but I didn't.

It's fear. When you have kids, even the littlest things become hazards. You look at the world through squinted eyes, always trying to imagine and prevent the worst. Electrical sockets and thumbtacks and stairs can be lethal. And that is when your children are born healthy. When they are not, it is almost too much. Bennett, this little one in my arms, needed surgery to repair an umbilical hernia when he was three months old. The pediatric surgeon who examined him after the surgery thought she saw the first signs of cranial synostosis, the premature fusion of the plates in his skull, which occurs more frequently in multiple births. It would mean corrective surgery as soon as possible. A CT scan showed that it was a false alarm, but this scare infected both Jennifer and me with a sort of paralysis, an overwhelming fear that things were never going to be normal again.

Bennett will be okay. I have to remember that. And I promise myself that I will call about the green-broke colt by noon the next day.

It's daylight now, and I've lost the newspaper ad. When I finally find it, I convince myself the colt has been sold already. I stare at the words, repeating them to myself. Green broke. $800. Will deliver. I pick up the phone, then put it down. I know I'm stalling. My excuse is that I don't want the horse to be trained. Green broke could mean anything. It could mean halter broke, sacked out, saddled, and ridden. I want to be the one who saddles the colt for the first time, to learn as he learns. I will probably only do this one time in my life, and I want to do it right. There will be other horses, I tell myself as I toss the ad in the trash.

Lord Jones, the Englishman on the Blue River, buys five hundred head of longhorn cows from a herd passing north from Texas. The cowboys who have trailed the herd don't know this country, so Teddy hires on to guide them. He is fifteen.

Teddy and the three Texas cowboys camp for the night

near a large prairie-dog town on the Blue. The prairie dogs chirp constantly, calling out alarms to each other. Back and forth, *chirp, chirp, chirp,* the entire night. All at once, the animals go quiet. Not just the prairie dogs, but the cattle and horses as well. Lightning flashes overhead and, in that white light, the men see the cows begin to run. The cowboys and Teddy mount their horses and race in circles, trying to contain the cows, to make the herd turn into itself and settle. The crash of thunder splits the sky. One man's shout is lost among the rumble of hooves. The cowboys spend hours chasing strays, circling the herd, and pushing it back to the edge of the river. Some of the cattle are lost. Teddy can hear them bawling away into the night. And one of the cowboys is missing as well, the one they call Pap. In the morning, they find him, broken, lying beside his horse. The man's saddle and saddle blanket and the handle of his revolver stick out from the bloody mash. The best Teddy and the other cowboys can figure, the horse stumbled in a prairie-dog hole and went down, taking Pap with him. The cattle milled over them the entire night.

Teddy and the others take turns digging with a broken-handled shovel. They scrape a shallow depression in the hillside and spread out Pap's tattered saddle blanket, then lay down his remains. They cover him with dirt and rocks. There is nothing they can do for the dead horse.

By the age of fifteen, Teddy has seen hundreds of dead cattle, five dead men not including his brother Jimmy, and too many dead horses. It is the cost of living on the plains, the price to be paid for trying to wrest a life from the land.

Teddy and the other cowboys gather the cattle and

drive them to Lord Jones's ranch along the Blue. The country is filled with Englishmen like Lord Jones, remittance men sent overseas with their trust funds to start a new life out west. Teddy thinks his father would have much in common with his fellow countrymen, but the old man can't stand to be around them.

After they run the last longhorn into the corrals, Teddy and the others tell Lord Jones what happened to Pap and ask if he will help them write a letter to Pap's parents back in Henrietta, Texas. *Your son was struck by lightning and we buried him in a nice spot along the Blue River.* It might have been true. It is the best they can do.

From the rack outside the hardware store, I take a copy of *Rocky Mountain Rider,* a free monthly horse-trading magazine. The newsprint pages list horse ranches with stallions available for breeding. Some ranches advertise purebred colts for sale. Charts map out pedigrees, showing each horse's sires and grandsires. I've never known anything about the bloodlines of the horses I've ridden. At best, each horse was a quarter horse or Appaloosa or paint. At worst, they were brown or black or bay. I've always figured, a horse is just a horse. Despite their pedigrees, all horses trace, eventually, back to an ugly, humpbacked animal that stood a foot tall and lived in the swamps fifty-five million years ago. This was Dawn Horse, the animal that evolved into the animal we know today.

When the colonists arrived in the New World, there were no horses to be found. Why they vanished is a mystery, but, by the tenth or eleventh century, they had disappeared from the land completely. Horses were reintroduced to the area when Spanish explorer Hernando Cortez invaded Mexico in 1519. Over the next two years, Cortez imported more than a thousand head. Twenty years later, another Spanish explorer, Hernando de Soto, imported more than two hundred horses for his expedition from the Everglades of Florida to the Missouri Ozarks. These horses were abandoned when the expedition ended and the men returned by river barge. At the same time, Francisco Vásquez de Coronado used horses to roam north from Mexico to what is now Nebraska and Kansas.

By the beginning of the seventeenth century, Native Americans were using horses for hunting and for war. Some historians believe the horses were taken from the huge bands of wild mustangs that roamed the Great Plains at that time, descendants of horses abandoned by the Spanish explorers. Others think the horses came from the missions that had been established in California and New Mexico. Whatever the source, the horse changed Indian life forever. Traditional hunting grounds were fair game to other tribes. War could be carried farther and faster than anyone could imagine.

Back east, the colonists imported two stallions and a half dozen mares to Jamestown in 1609. Draft breeds were used by the colonists of Pennsylvania, but smaller horses were preferred in the south, for riding around plantations and for sport. Quarter-mile tracks were carved out of the timbered hills of Maryland, Virginia, and the Carolinas as horse racing grew in popularity. The most successful horses were those with quick bursts of speed. These winning steeds were bred to each other and eventually the first uniquely American breed, the quarter horse, was developed almost a century before the advent of Thoroughbreds.

Thoroughbreds trace their origins to King Charles II, ruler of England from 1660 to 1685. Charles imported three stallions of Arabian, Turkish, and Barbary descent, and bred them to native English "running horses." The resulting offspring had large nostrils and deep, narrow chests for increased lung capacity. Their features were refined, thin-skinned, graceful.

I page through the *Rocky Mountain Rider,* thinking about bloodlines and history, about the features that define us. I wonder if what we carry in our blood and bones is all we have, or if we are somehow able to overcome our pedigrees. And then an ad catches my eye:

> HORSES! HUGE CHOICE, ALL TYPES, BREEDS.
> KID-SAFE TO GOOD TRAIL STOCK.
> STANDING AQHA, APHA, TB STALLION.

There is a local phone number at the bottom. Something about the ad, maybe it's the exclamation point after "horses," makes me think this is the place. Horses!

A woman's voice on the answering machine tells me to leave a message. I hang up. Maybe Bob Ricketts will sell me a horse to train. He raises Oberlanders. The name reminds me of a shop teacher I had back in high school. Mr. Oberlander. Christ, I'm stalling again. There's a horse ranch up on Sunny Slope Hill, north of town. Milliron paint horses.

I think they have a production sale every April, where they auction off colts. That might work. Everyone loves a paint, the flashy brown or black against white. I've never ridden a paint. I'd probably look good riding one.

Horses!

I try the phone number again.

"Hello?" It is the soft, small voice of a man expecting more bad news.

"I saw your ad that says you have horses for sale," I say. "I was wondering if you have anything that hasn't been trained?"

"Yeah, I do," he says. "I've got a coming two. Real nice roan. And then I got another gelding, a coming three, he's a little sorrel. We can surely find you something. Who am I talking to?"

I tell him my name and where I live.

"Oh you're real close then," he says. "We're down here where the highway makes the corner. The house is the very last place on Spring Creek Lane. It's called a lane, you know, because it doesn't go anywhere else."

"Would you mind getting together sometime, to show me those horses?" I ask.

"We have Bible study in the morning," he says. "But any time after noon is good."

Only a handful of horse ranches remain in the valley. Since I lost my job on the ranch, my life has been narrowed down to the few miles from home to the grocery store in town. But I know this man. I've watched from afar as he and his sons feed their horses hay in the winter. Watched one of his sons ride his horse along the shoulder of the highway, heading up into the mountains. Seen their red Ford pickup and old blue stock trailer parked at McDonald's. They have been an escape for me. I've studied them, envied them, imagined what it would be like to be in their cowboy boots and under their hats, riding their horses. Now is my chance to find out.

The colt is stretching his head under the bottom wire, trying to reach a clump of orchard grass, when he sees the big brown horse move along the other side of the fence, between the pasture and the lake. This strange horse browses on last year's cattails. It dips its huge nose into the pooled water at its feet and drinks. At the sound of a motorcycle accelerating on the straight stretch of highway, the animal startles.

The colt bobs his head up and down across the top wire and whinnies at the loose horse. He trots along the fence line, tail held high. But he stops in his tracks when the breeze comes off the lake from the north. The colt can smell that it isn't a horse at all. Like the bears that sometimes wander through the pasture in the spring and fall, or the coyotes that slink through on their way to something better, this thing carries the smell of wildness. Aspen leaves and musk, rotten wood and running water. The colt watches the moose amble toward the lake on his impossibly long legs, then stares at the spot where it disappears into a clump of alders. When he is certain it is gone for good, the colt bends down and tries to graze on the other side of the fence once again.

Sunday afternoon. I turn off the highway and follow Spring Creek Lane south. After a quarter mile the road bends left, toward the mountains. Junked cars and trucks and boats line the lane. I pass a huge crane, horse trailers, snowmobiles. The one-story house is sided in coffee-colored wood. Down a small hill below the house, I see some ramshackle sheds, a small barn, and a muddy corral. A set of rough wooden steps leads up to the front door and the men are standing there, not talking, when I pull up and park. I get out of the truck.

The cowboy is in his late fifties. He wears a red bandanna tied around his neck. A white T-shirt peeks out from under his blue denim shirt. He shakes my hand and gives me his business card, black ink in an old Western font printed on tan paper. In the center of the card, the man's initials are linked together to form his brand next to the word HORSES in large, bold letters. Below, in the left corner, are his name, address, and phone number. The right corner of the card has a drawing of a trio of horses with the words THREE STALLIONS printed below.

"This is my boy, Clay," the man says, pointing at the silent red-haired thirty-year-old alongside him. They both have the short, wiry stature of bull riders. "I got eight boys altogether," the man says proudly. In person, the man's timid phone voice grows stronger. "You got time for coffee?" I nod and follow them up the porch steps.

Inside, the house is a cowboy bachelor pad. There's a case of motor oil on a kitchen chair, dirty winter boots on the carpet. The mounted head of a huge bull elk hangs on the far wall, next to a hand-painted sign with a variation of a Harry S. Truman quip: NEVER KICK A FRESH TURD ON A HOT DAY.

Clay and I sit at the kitchen table. A loaded dishwasher gapes open and plastic bowls of brown eggs line the counter. On the table in front of me, there is a dirty coffee mug with a red rose and the name DELORES printed on it. I remember the voice on the answering machine. Eight sons. The woman must have died from exhaustion. I think of what it must be like to lose your partner in life and not be able to give up the things they left behind.

"Gotta have fresh coffee," the man says, pouring water into the machine. "The good thing about a Bunn is that it brews fresh in the time it takes to reheat cold. Now, tell me a little about how much you're looking to spend."

"As little as possible," I say.

He laughs and gives me a brief lesson in the economics of raising horses. "And so," he summarizes, "I figure I got five hundred dollars a year into each horse. And that's not even taking into consideration the fact that not all of the mares get bred every year, and not all of the foals make it. If I was to register my horses, that'd be another four hunnerd right there."

The pitch feels a little weak to me, like it's been worn out on other buyers. He wants a thousand dollars for a two-year-old, fifteen hundred for a three. Maybe I should just walk away now, before I drink a cup of coffee and feel like I owe him. I could make a phone call and find out more about that green-broke colt. He was only eight hundred dollars. On the kitchen wall above the coffeemaker there is a bouquet of plastic flowers with a card that reads GET OVER IT.

"Tell me," the man asks, "why do you want to train a horse yourself?"

I don't know how to answer. I look out the window to the mountains, at Delores's bone-colored mug on the table, at my hands in my lap.

"Because you want to," he says, pouring coffee into two cups. He smiles. "Clay, why don't you go catch up Frito and Cletus and we'll be down to look them over in a bit." Clay gets up from his seat and ambles out the door.

A pickup drives into the yard. The man looks at the Regulator wall clock and says, "That must be the folks here to look at 4-H pigs." We leave the coffee and walk outside together, and for a second, I feel like another son, out to do the day's chores. The man getting out of the truck is a heavyset Indian. He hitches up his jeans and we walk down to the pigpen together, just beyond the muddy corral below the house. Clay is in the corral, halter in hand, trying to trap a roan colt in the corner.

The man buying the weaner pigs asks a lot of questions—how much weight the pigs will gain, what he should feed them—before admitting, "I don't know the first thing about hogs." This honesty causes me to snap out of my dream that I am the cowboy's son. I am more like the man buying an animal for a project, something for the kids. At least he has 4-H as an excuse, which is more than I have. He pays fifty dollars for three pigs. "I'll be back to pick them up on Saturday," he says, before driving off.

The cowboy pockets the check and we walk over to the corrals together. "There's the Thoroughbred stud I use," he says, pointing to a beautiful black horse in a small pen. "Some of the horses we raised ourselves, others I've traded for. This one here is Cletus." He walks up to the roan colt which Clay has caught and tied to the corral rail. "He's the two-year-old." The horse heaves back on his rope at our approach. The corral post creaks, threatening to snap. The man stops and turns to his son, asking, "What's the deal, Clay?"

Clay shrugs, his mirrored wraparound sunglasses reflecting the mud at his feet.

The man unties the horse slowly, surely, whispering to it, telling him everything is all right. He tips his cowboy hat back on his head, the weak March sun hitting his pale forehead. He blows softly into the horse's nostrils. "It seems to calm them," he says, "once they get a whiff of you." He hands me the rope. "Why don't you walk him around a little."

I lead the horse around the corral, the mud like brown oatmeal sucking at our feet. I stop and face the colt. I draw imaginary lines down the animal's front legs, back legs, hindquarters, trying to remember what makes a good horse. Conformation. The illustrations of the ideal.

"He likes you," the man says. "And I can see that you've got patience. Training a horse is like raising kids. You need to be patient, firm, and kind. You want Clay to saddle him up for you?"

If Clay can saddle him, I can't buy this horse. I want to

do it all, from the beginning. I don't want to compromise on this point. "Do you have something that hasn't been saddled yet?" I ask.

"Let's take a look at Frito," the man says, reaching out so that I'll hand him Cletus's rope.

Though he is a full year older than the roan, Frito is smaller. I'm no expert, but even I can tell he's a sorry-looking horse. He's got a big head and a swayback and a long tail. All of his ribs are there. Everything seems out of proportion. Pieces of his hide are missing on one side, and there is a raw scrape down his nose. God, I feel bad for him. I love an underdog, but I can't buy this horse either.

"He'll fill out some," the man says, "but he'll never be as big as that other." I take the rope and lead Frito around the corral anyway. I stop and pet his neck. I silently apologize to the colt. I'm sorry.

"Has he been handled much?" I ask.

The man turns to his son. "You've ridden him, haven't you, Clay?"

"A little."

"They're real nice horses," I say, giving him back the lead rope. "But I better think about it."

Up the hill, outside the house, the man is ready to get on with his day. I've disappointed him. Another deadbeat buyer. Another cup of coffee wasted. Buckets of oats and bales of hay are loaded in the back of his flatbed Ford. He shakes my hand and asks, "Did I give you my card?"

I nod, then ask, "You're sure you don't have anything else on the place?"

He scratches his chin. "There's some fillies across the road, coming twos. Maybe one of them would work for you?"

"I really wanted a gelding," I admit, "but a filly might work." I look at the bales stacked on the flatbed truck. "I know you have work to do."

"Clay and me are going over there to feed anyway," he says. "Why don't you follow in your truck?"

We drive down the lane, turn right onto the highway, then travel just fifty yards before turning off on a little dirt road. We rattle across a cattle guard and head toward the lake. Horses run in the field, knowing it's lunchtime. At the barbed wire fence, the man takes a five-gallon bucket of grain and scatters it away from the wire gate, to draw the horses from the opening. Clay drives through. I park my truck and follow on foot, closing the gate behind me.

"Be careful," the man calls out, swatting at a horse with the empty bucket. "One of my boys got kicked not so long ago. Took a hoof to the ribs." He takes another bucket from the bed of the truck and scatters a wake of oats through the short spring grass. When the buckets are empty, he takes a pocketknife, cuts the strings on the bales, and flakes hay off the back of the truck as Clay drives. I walk alongside, watching the horses eat. "There's a nice filly there," the man says, stabbing in the direction of a little bay with the blade of his knife.

"What about that gelding?" I ask, pointing to a big shaggy buckskin.

"Yeah, I'd sell him to you. That's Dillon. He's got hazel eyes. I never seen anything like it. He's what you call warm-blooded. Part draft horse and part Thoroughbred. We call him Dillon because, on *Gunsmoke*, Matt Dillon always rode a big buckskin."

I stand fifteen feet from the horse, studying him. There isn't anything obviously wrong with him. I look into his eyes, which glow amber across the distance, and try to imagine a future with this horse.

"And there's another gelding over here," the man calls out, pointing to a colt eating hay alone. He is dark brown, his hide turning lighter at his muzzle. He is the color of Festus's mule. "He's a fall colt, coming three this year," the man says. "We call him 'Black,' because when he was younger, he was pure black. As you can see, he isn't really black anymore."

The colt watches us as it eats. His eyes are dark brown. There is a little band of white above his right rear hoof. Behind me, horses squeal as they fight over a hay pile, but the brown colt doesn't flinch.

Clay gets out of the truck and closes the door, his hands in the pockets of his jeans.

I feel as if I've run out of excuses. Even my insistence on finding an untrained horse is starting to wear a little thin. If I'm going to do it, either of these horses will work. "Have they been handled much?"

The man looks over to Clay, who shrugs.

"Well, Clay," the man asks, "have you ridden them?"

His son hesitates, then says no, almost as if he thinks he's in trouble for not having worked the colts.

"We better drive out of here while the horses are still eating," the man says, "otherwise they'll try to follow us out." He gets in the truck and drives, while Clay and I walk to the gate. The truck pulls through and Clay latches it closed. The man turns off the truck and gets out and we stand around the flatbed, one man to a side, like it is a conference table.

"What do you need to get out of those horses?" I ask. This is always the hardest part for me, the bargaining.

"I suppose I can let you have Dillon for fifteen hunnerd, or that Black for twelve."

I look back to the horses, trying to spot the buckskin or the brown. There's a three-hundred-dollar difference in their prices and probably more than that in their worth. The big buckskin is fit and flashy, the little brown colt looks a bit forlorn. I remember an old saying: "One white foot, buy 'em. Two white feet, try 'em. Three white feet, be on the sly. Four white feet, pass 'em by." I'm not sure what any of it is based on, a folktale or superstition, but it's enough to help me decide.

"I'll take the black one," I say. "Is it okay if I pay you now and pick him up in a week or so, when I figure out where I'm going to keep him?"

"I think that'd be a fine idea," the man says, smiling. "He can stay here for a week or two, but I just lost the lease on this pasture. The Tribe is taking it back because they say they want to restore it as a wetlands area. I have to get these horses out of here by the end of the month. But we can keep him around the house there. Or, if you want to keep him with us, we've got some pasture up on Turtle Lake Road. I'd do that for seventy-five a month."

"I'll see what I can line up on my own and get back to you," I say, taking the checkbook from my back pocket.

The man smiles. "You and Clay can work your horses together. He likes company." I look over at Clay, who is grinning now behind his mirrored sunglasses. "You should see him down there, singing to the horses," the man says. "It does my heart good. When your horse is ready, you can go riding up into the mountains together."

I sign my name on the check and hand it to the man. "Do we need a bill of sale?"

"Here it is," the man says, holding out his right hand. He means a handshake is good enough.

"For the brand inspector," I say. "Doesn't the state need something in writing?"

"Yeah," the man says. "I guess so. I don't think that colt's been branded, but you'll have to get him inspected anyhow. I can give you the names of some guys to call about getting that done. Did I give you my card?"

I nod, then turn back for one last look at the colt, but he's disappeared into the rest of the herd.

✯ ✯ ✯

At night, he pens the cattle. During the day, he lets them out to graze. The neighbors pay him a dollar fifty per head for six months of care. He is sixteen years old, and the work and the wages give Teddy a dangerous independence. He spends his free time in Lincoln, and the Texas cowboys who pass through fill his head with stories of life on the trail. He dreams of nothing else. He buys guns and whiskey. He pays the man at the studio on Q Street to take his photograph. His right hand rests on his knee. His left hand holds a whiskey bottle. An unlit cigar balances between his lips. His wide-brimmed hat is tilted back, exposing a white forehead. And his wide eyes are hooded, daring you to call him a kid.

He loves it, this life. He loves the hard work and the way that first drink of whiskey tastes. He loves his horse though, in all honesty, it is really his father's. Teddy longs to follow the herds north, to escape his father, and the old man's constant disappointment.

Teddy keeps the photograph tucked in the pages of his Bible back in his room at home, because he knows it will be safe there. The book goes unused. If there is nothing more in this life than horses and cigars and whiskey and cattle, it's fine with Teddy. He couldn't be happier.

★　★　★

After four rings, the answering machine clicks on. It's the voice of a maniacal Norwegian grandmother shouting, "Ya, thanks for calling. I am out making some chan-ges in my life. If I don't return your call, you are one of the chan-ges." I hang up, get the phone book, check the number, and dial again. Same message.

"Hi, Bob, this is Tom Groneberg," I say. "I hope I have the right number. I just bought a colt and was wondering if, like we talked about, I could bring him out to your place. Give me a call back and let me know."

A week passes without a word from Bob, and I begin to wonder how serious he is about making changes in his life.

Maybe I am one of the changes. I made a huge mistake. I bought a horse without a place to keep him. The colt is a living, breathing being, not a project I can mothball in the garage. I've added another thing to my life that requires care, when there are already too many things to care for.

I take the business card from under the refrigerator magnet and call the man I bought the colt from. I think about asking him to forget the whole thing. Maybe it isn't too late to cancel the check. I can pay him something for his trouble and never look back.

He picks up on the fourth ring and, at the sound of his voice, I lose my nerve.

"Umm, well, I'm having some trouble lining up a place to pasture the horse," I tell him. "Is it all right if I leave him with you for another month?"

"Sure," he says. "That'll be fine. We said seventy-five a month?"

"Yes," I say. "That's great."

"You can just drop off a check at the house if I'm not around."

Seventy-five dollars. That would pay for some new clothes for the boys. I could buy Jennifer something nice with that money, something to thank her for taking such good care of our family. But instead, I'm spending it on grass for a horse. I remember trying to explain to Jennifer why I wanted to buy a colt. "I want something of my own," I told her, "something that's just for me. I know it sounds selfish."

"It's a little selfish," she said, "but it's okay to be selfish sometimes. I just want you to be okay."

I drive down the lane and pull up to the house. With all of the vehicles around, it's hard to tell which ones are drivers and which are junkers. I walk past them, up the rough lumber steps and knock on the front door. A short woman with a dishwater blond ponytail opens the door.

"I'm dropping off a check for a month of pasture for a colt I just bought," I explain.

"Oh, okay," she says. "I'll make sure he gets it. Him and the boys are hauling horses." I realize she must be Delores, come back from the grave. I imagined her dead from exhaustion after raising eight sons, her heartbroken husband unable to let her go. I hand her the check and shamble down the crooked steps, back to my truck.

★　★　★

The little brown colt and four other horses are loaded into a stock trailer and driven two miles south to the pasture on Turtle Lake Road. The truck stops, the gate swings open, and the horses step down from the trailer onto grass clipped short by the brood mares already grazing there. Before the colt can even get his bearings, a paint runs at him, spins, and kicks him in the ribs. The colt turns, but she bites him on the rear as he flees, chasing him to the far corner of the field. A smaller sorrel gelding tries to bite the colt, but he doesn't back down and they spend the next three hours sparring. The colt hasn't had time to eat, and the hollow feeling in his gut is as big and as blue as the sky above. He settles in next to the big buckskin with the golden eyes, keeping himself as far away from the paint mare as he can.

"I just got back into the country." It's Bob's voice and the static from his cell phone singing through the receiver. "It was spring break, so I loaded the kids into the travel trailer and drove down to Arizona to see the grandma, then over to Disneyland. Thirty-five hundred miles in seven days. And I don't drink."

I laugh at his description and from the feeling of relief that comes over me. "So that's where you were," I say.

"Let me hear about your colt."

I tell him as much as I know, which doesn't take long.

"Well," he says, "we'll have to make sure he's been vaccinated and wormed and had his West Nile shot. Then he'll fit right in with my horses. When you want to move him?"

"I don't have a trailer," I say. "But I'm looking at a little two-horse bumper pull that's for sale."

"That one parked out on the highway?" Bob asks.

"Yeah, you've seen it? They want eight hundred for it."

"Hell, don't buy that," he says. "I don't want to tell you what to do, but don't do that. We'll just use my trailer. It's a four-horse slant load and when it comes to horses, bigger is always better. Save your money. You can have some time to look for something a little more handy than that two-horse. When you want to move him?"

"Any time you can do it," I tell him. "My truck doesn't have a gooseneck hitch, though."

"We'll use mine then."

"And the colt isn't broke, so it might turn into a rodeo."

"I'll bring some extra rope," he says. "We'll get him in. I'll call you sometime next week and let you know how things are shaping up. I've got a foal and mare I need to haul to the vet's in Ronan next week, so maybe we can do it then."

"I'll find out what shots he's had and make sure he's good," I tell him.

"We'll talk to you later then."

"Bob?" I pause. "Thanks."

"Well, it's no big thing," he says. "And congratulations on your colt."

Next I phone the man whom I bought the colt from and ask him about getting a brand inspector to write up a bill of sale. He gives me the names and numbers of a few people to try. Then I ask about his vaccination program.

"We don't give anything and we've never had any troubles," he says. "We just sold a dozen mares and had them tested for everything and they came out clean. We've never had any trouble a-tall."

Anymore, I'm a believer in vaccinations and insurance and anything else you can do to try to minimize regret. When Jennifer was pregnant, she had the usual screening tests and they all came back fine. We could have opted for an amniocentesis, but there was a risk of miscarriage with that procedure, and with twins, the risk doubled. An amnio would probably have told us that Baby A had Down syndrome. Currently, when expectant parents hear that diagnosis, they terminate the pregnancy nine out of ten times. In my heart I know that since there were two babies, we never would have chosen that. But had we known about Avery's condition sooner, we would have had time to prepare, to learn more about Down syndrome.

Avery has trisomy 21. He's got three—rather than two—chromosomes making up the twenty-first pair of chromosomes in every cell of his body. No one is sure why it happens. What is certain is this: Avery is mentally retarded, he is sterile, and—if he follows the national average for people with Down syndrome—he will live to be fifty. I remind myself that I wanted our twins to be as different as possible. We bypassed the safe, mirrored world of identical twins, and entered an altogether different place.

Teddy spends five hundred dollars he's earned on three horses, a tent, a bedroll, a gun, and a girl. The girl, who lives in Lincoln, doesn't last. Teddy uses the new horses to help move the cattle he's tended the last four months to the feedlots in eastern Nebraska. The sorrel is a nice horse, light on his feet, but—given the chance—he has a habit of tipping Teddy's hat off his head. The dark bay steps out like he's walking in mud. He's not worth much, and Teddy will trade him off at the first opportunity. The blood bay is not to be trusted.

When Teddy returns from the east, his father tells him, "You can take old Morgan and Kit and Charlie and plow the west ridge tomorrow." Teddy is a cowboy now. He doesn't think much of farmers. His father and his brothers can plow and plant and wait for the sun and the rain; Teddy is going to punch cows.

He drifts, moving west along the Platte River, herding cattle north to the Pine Ridge Reservation in South Dakota, then south to Austin, Texas. There, he hires on with the Olive Ranch. They're moving a herd up the Western Trail to Nebraska. Teddy's heard the tales of the gunfights and merciless beatings dealt out by the Olive outfit, and he wants to prove his own toughness. He wants a reputation, wants to use his Colt to show that he is a bigger man than his body allows. He is eighteen years old, living a life he'd only dreamed about. He doesn't think much about what he left behind.

There are eleven cowboys and a cook who travels with the wagon. Teddy gets paid a dollar a day. They are moving two thousand longhorn steers and four dozen horses. At Doane's Crossing, they ford the Red, leaving Texas for the Indian Nations, then Kansas and Nebraska. Outside of Dodge City, Teddy rides to the top of a hill, scouting for a runaway steer. Below him, he sees the dust rising from two herds ahead of the Olive outfit, and three behind. On the other side of the river, he sees seven more herds. Thousands upon thousands of cattle. Hundreds of horses and men. All moving north. It is so beautiful to him.

When the cattle are turned over in Nebraska, the cowboys draw their wages. Teddy rides into North Platte and spends ten dollars on a large, white Stetson, twelve for new pants, eight for a shirt. He buys boots with red and blue stovepipe shafts, inlaid stars, and a crescent moon. They are the first clothes he has ever purchased from a store.

He heads east to the place on Haines Branch. He's been gone a year and hasn't written or sent word in that time. He didn't have any news to share with them anyhow. When he arrives, his father won't even look at him. His sister makes fun of his new clothes. "Take your pants out of your boots and put your coat on," she says. "You look like an outlaw." But these are the first clothes he's ever worn that weren't sewn by his mother. It doesn't matter what they think. He loves his new boots and he is proud of his new self. He has made his own way in the world and, though they can't see it, he has become a man. He has everything he needs without them. The sky is at his feet.

A wooden ladder propped on the porch leads up to the roof, where a television antenna is perched like an aluminum skeleton reaching for the sky. The roof is peaked like the mountains in the background, like the straw cowboy hat on the man's head. He is there waiting for me when I pull down the lane. His blue jeans are tucked into brown leather cowboy boots. He's wearing that faded salesman's smile. "The brand inspector never made it," he says.

"I told him ten-thirty," I say, closing the door of my truck.

"Oh, I thought you said ten." He checks his watch. "Well, then, there's still time. Who'd you call?"

"I got ahold of Trevor. He was the only one who could come."

"Trevor's good. He'll be here." He jerks a thumb over his shoulder. "Clay's just brushing some beggar's lice out of your horse's mane." I follow the man over to where the colt is tied to an old swather, a machine used for cutting hay. The swather is a Hesston, its red paint faded lipstick pink, just like the one I owned back on the ranch in Miles City. A Wisconsin air-cooled engine. The serrated teeth of the cutting bar, rotting with rust and age. I can hear it, even now.

"I need to get rid of some of these old junkers," the man says, waving his arms at the broken-down cars and trucks and trailers lining the lane, as if he is performing a magic act, as if he can make them disappear. Twin Cadillac Sedan DeVilles are parked next to each other, mirror images, with identical piles of white chicken crap on the dark blue hoods. Riding lawn mowers, snowmobiles, boats. The giant crane reaching into the sky.

"The boys always think they are going to fix them up, so I just leave them sit," he explains.

I begin to see the place in a new light. Maybe it is a shift in the clouds or a trick played by the sun, but instead of a junkyard filled with worthless scrap metal and seized pistons, I now see rusty hope and opportunity. A long-dead engine that might be started. The promise of something better. A chance at a new life.

"Tell me again," the man asks, "where are you taking the horse?"

"You know Bob Ricketts?"

The man nods.

"I'm meeting him at eleven out on the highway and we're going to use his trailer to haul the horse up to his place on the west shore."

"I know he's hooked up with Forrest Davis, and that they do those carriage rides together," he says. "He'll tell you a lot about horses. More than he probably knows, if you get what I'm saying."

The cry of a strange bird rises from down behind the pigpens, and the man turns at the sound. He takes a toothpick from the black ribbon that encircles his cowboy hat, and chews on it thoughtfully.

I study the colt. He looks skinny, ribby, his brown hair shedding in clumps. For a second, I think that maybe they've switched horses on me. But there is the little white band just above his right rear hoof. He's a shadow of the animal I remember buying. The colt stands tied to the swather without pulling back or lunging forward. He looks completely tame. Maybe, after I turned down the first two horses he showed me, the man just said this horse was green. There must have been some wink or nod between him and his son, or maybe they talked it over in the pickup on their way out to feed that afternoon. *Now when I ask you if you've worked the horse, just don't answer.* I remember the way Clay hesitated before he answered, which made me think he was in trouble. Maybe he was giving himself away. Maybe he is a bad liar.

The man looks down to the corrals below the house, to the where the sound of the shrieking bird rises. The toothpick works in his mouth. "I'll be right back," he says. And I am left alone with Clay and the colt.

There is a story in my family about one of my grandfather's brothers, Uncle Ernst, a Minnesota farmer who was unburdened by scruples when it came to trading horses. One day a farmer visited Ernst, hoping to buy a workhorse. "I got one for ya," Ernst said, "and I give you a deal, because that horse, he don't look too good." The farmer examined the animal in question. The horse was a little rough, the farmer thought, but it looked fit enough to pull a plow, and the price was right. He paid Ernst and led the horse away. But when he got home, the farmer discovered the animal was completely blind. Outraged, the farmer demanded his money back from Ernst, who only smiled and said, "I told ya, that horse don't look too good."

I'm not sure if this story is true, but it has me wondering. Careful not to scare the colt, I reach up slowly and run my hand in front of his eyes. He blinks, one side, then the other. Clay stops his brushing and stares at me. I pick one of the tiny white burrs from the colt's mane and smile at Clay. I try to remember if his father gave me any similar disclaimers, anything that might hint at the colt's faults. Maybe it isn't too late to call this whole thing off. But I paid for the colt. I shook the man's hand and, out here, that means it's a done deal. If this is a mistake, it is my mistake, and I need to own it.

After Jennifer and I decided to have another child, there was never any point at which I said yes or no that could have changed anything. Here is my chance to make the right decision, and I'm not sure this colt, or any horse for that matter, is the right thing to choose.

I watch Clay, the cowboy's son, as he brushes the colt. I think of Avery. At nine months old, he isn't sitting up. He

can't crawl. He is smaller than Bennett, a difference I feel
each time I pick them up. Avery is weightless, grounded,
a hollow-boned bird. He seems incomplete. Once, I took
his face in my hands. I reshaped his eyes, pulling them
down, trying to mold him to look like his brothers, his
mother, or me. But it didn't change him, it only made me
feel ashamed of myself. He is who he is. He is my son.

Clay stops brushing the colt. He's looking down the
lane at the truck coming toward us. It's Trevor, the brand
inspector. We fill out the paperwork on the colt. The
man is here, now, handing his business card to Trevor and
telling him, "Call me if you ever need a horse." I tell the
man I'll be back in an hour or two with a trailer.

At the highway, parked at the turnout to Turtle Lake
Road, is a silver-and-white Dodge pickup hooked to a
bright yellow trailer with blue and red lettering that
reads: WORLD FAMOUS OBERLANDER HORSES. Behind the
trailer, a tribal policeman sits in his black truck, talking
into a radio. I park my truck and walk up to the Dodge.
With his seat reclined and black felt cowboy hat over his
eyes, Bob is taking a nap.

"You snuck up on me," he says from under the hat.

"It looks like you got pulled over. There's a tribal cop
behind you."

"That's all right," he says. "My trailer registration is
only expired by a few years." He sits upright and puts his
hat back on his head. "We all set?"

"Yes," I say. "The brand inspector came and filled out
the paperwork on the colt. We're all ready to go."

Bob looks at his Mickey Mouse wristwatch. Mickey's

hands point to eleven-thirty. "If you want to get those shots from the vet, they close at noon for lunch, so we better head over there now," he says. "And we can call Forrest and see if he wants to meet up and grab something to eat. But we should take your truck so we don't have to drag this trailer to hell and back."

We get in my truck and drive west along the south shore of the lake, past the old San Francisco Ranch and the Wal-Mart and the Safeway, to the junction with Highway 93, then south, to Ronan. I dip my hand into a bag of sunflower seeds, pop a few in my mouth, roll down the window, and chew and spit hulls out into the Montana day. I offer Bob some seeds, but he shakes his head no and chews his gum. It's got an odd smell to it, and I imagine it must be some old-time flavor, like Clove gum or Blackjack.

"I forgot to ask you about your answering machine," I say, remembering the voice of the Norwegian grandma on Bob's outgoing message.

He laughs. "It isn't original, but it works to weed out the people you don't want to talk to. It's helped me with a few old girlfriends."

I head up Polson Hill, then turn off the highway into the parking lot of the veterinarian's office. Inside, I stand at the counter while the vet's assistant prepares two doses of West Nile vaccine, one for now and one to give in a month. I also get a dose of wormer and a five-way vaccine. Bob is chatting with someone in an examination room, trying to get them to take a pair of goats off his hands, but it doesn't sound like he's getting anywhere. "They're real docile," he says, "and they'll control the weeds in your pastures.

Maybe I can just drop them off at your place some day." I hear a woman laugh and Bob says, "Well, if you change your mind, just let me know." Then we are back in the pickup, the vaccines wrapped in a plastic baggie with an ice pack to keep them cool.

Bob takes out his cell phone and punches in a few numbers. "Forrest Davis!" he yells. "Let's get some lunch. Meet you at the Pizza Café in ten minutes."

After he hangs up, I tell Bob about Tim, my old boss. "He used to log with horses in the North Fork, and Forrest would help him out when he had problems."

"Forrest has taught me so much," Bob says. "Did I ever tell you about the St. Patrick's Day parade in Butte? I was driving a delivery wagon pulled by one horse down the street, when everything went to hell. And I remember Forrest always telling me, if your horses blow up, run them into something big and solid and do it quick before someone gets hurt. I picked a Trans Am. A news crew from ABC caught it on tape. I'll have to show it to you sometime."

"Tim figured Forrest was probably gone by now," I say.

"He just turned eighty-one." Bob takes a blister pack of large square pills from his shirt pocket, peels back a bit of foil, and pops one in his mouth. He starts chewing. It's nicotine gum. "I have to warn you about one thing," Bob says.

"What's that?"

"Forrest can be awful blunt sometimes. He doesn't have time to figure out how to say something without hurting a person's feelings." Bob puts the pack of gum back in his shirt pocket. "Once Forrest was hauling some canner horses for that woman over at the animal sanctuary. She'd bought them at auction and was pretty proud that she'd saved them from slaughter. She asked Forrest what he'd do with the horses if they were his. He looked the gal in the eye and told her, 'I'd can 'em.'"

I laugh.

"I'll tell you another thing. When I first met Forrest, I had a hunch he was getting pissed off at me, but I couldn't figure out why. And then it dawned on me that I was talking too much. I'm Irish. I have the gift of gab." He shrugs. It's something that can't be helped. "So after I figured that out, I started counting the number of words he'd use when showing me something. And I'd ask him a question using the same number of words. After a while, he started to warm up to me."

The colt stands tied to the swather, both fading in the early May sun. The young horse's legs are stiff from standing in one spot. Except for the big black dog sleeping on the front porch, the colt is alone. He listens to the raucous call of the guinea hen, smells the sweet manure of hogs on the breeze.

He is thirsty. He is hungry. He is tired.

He hears the swoosh of wings beating the air above. A shadow passes across the sheet metal of the swather. An eagle soaring overhead, playing on the thermals.

With his lips, the colt works on the lead rope, trying to pull the end of the slipknot free, but he only manages to get the slack of the rope caught on a bolt protruding from the sheet metal of the machine. The colt can hear the gargle of the creek that flows through the place and he day-dreams of water.

We sit at a table away from the front door. The waitress brings menus and glasses of ice water. Outside, I can see the fairgrounds where the county rodeo is held each July. The bucking chutes and the grandstands are silent and empty today. I know Bob has ridden bareback horses in local rodeos. At Bob's store, there is a print of a pencil drawing, framed and hanging on one of the walls. It is titled *Bob's Last Ride* and shows him coming out of a bucking chute on the back of a bronc. Below is the caption, "48, Going on 17, Looking for 8."

I remember the saddle bronc I rode in the Miles City Bucking Horse Sale. It's the largest event in southeast Montana, held each year during the third weekend in May. I rode in the sale seven years ago. At the time, I told myself I was riding so that I could have a horse story of my own to tell. Now, I think it was just a desperate attempt to fit in with the local ranch hands and cowboys. It didn't work. I'm afraid I've done the same thing in buying the colt.

"Have you ever been to the Bucking Horse Sale in Miles City?" I ask.

"I went one year with Forrest," Bob says. "It's a long way down there. What is it, six hundred miles?"

"Something like that. It's coming up in another two weeks."

"We hauled down a wagon and a team for the parade. I brought my rigging and was going to ride in the sale, but Forrest wouldn't let me. He dressed me down in front of a lot of people. Said the horses were too wild and I had better things to get busted up over." He takes a sip of water and looks up. "There he is now."

A white, late-model Chevy pickup pulls into the parking lot. It's got four doors and dual rear wheels. The truck comes to a stop on the fresh gravel farthest from the front door of the café. "He has handicap stickers because of his new knees, but he never uses the spot up front," Bob says. "Maybe he wants the exercise. Did I tell you he's almost been killed off three times?"

I shake my head.

"Yeah, but he'll outlive you and me both."

The little old man walks across the gravel using a cane.

"Does he ever like to be helped?" I ask.

"That is a very good question," Bob says gravely. "If you stay quiet, he'll ask for help when he needs it. With me, he has this routine where he's the foreman and I'm the hired hand. He'll boss me around, and I let him."

The door to the restaurant opens and Bob shouts "Forrest Davis!" across the dining room. The old man raises his head and nods and works his way over to our table. He wears a straw cowboy hat, blue suspenders, and thermal underwear beneath his long-sleeved shirt. His faded jeans have been cut vertically on each side of the waist, and darker denim has been added to let out the waist. He's not at all what I thought he'd be. Mustache, hearing aid, white hair barely tamed under the sweat-stained hat. He looks like Albert Einstein's cowboy brother.

Bob says, "Forrest, Tom. Tom, Forrest Davis." We shake hands, then study the menus and order lunch. Bob gets a salad "with a lot of blue cheese dressing." Forrest orders fish-and-chips, "without the chips," and a bowl of chicken tortilla soup. I choose a cheeseburger and fries.

"Tom lived in Miles City a while back," Bob says. "We were just talking about the time you wouldn't let me ride in the Bucking Horse Sale."

A look of mild disgust shades the old man's face. "You were forty-seven, forty-eight. You have three kids. You should have known better."

"But I had the right attitude," Bob offers.

"Doesn't mean shit."

I keep my mouth shut for most of the meal, taking to heart Bob's warning about talking too much. The men discuss draft horses, different hitches and configurations of teams, things I know nothing about. "You need to teach me the four-up before you die," Bob says. Forrest nods, as if they've talked about this before.

"Tom here just bought a colt," Bob says, and he tells Forrest where I got him.

Forrest looks up from his chipless fish. "Then he's wormy," he says. "Make sure you worm him good." Bob and I exchange looks. "That guy never registers his colts," Forrest says, "and he doesn't show anyone the papers on his stallions or mares. But your colt should have a lot of Dash for Cash in his blood."

I'm pretty sure Dash for Cash was a quarter horse sire back in the seventies. History passed down through the blood. Dawn Horse living in the swamps millions of years ago. Here, then gone, then back again. Wild mustangs, quarter horses, Thoroughbreds, all a prologue to a wormy little colt, my horse.

We finish our lunch. I suppress the urge to take Forrest's elbow as he navigates the tables and chairs of the dining room on his way to the door.

Outside I say, "It was great meeting you, Mr. Davis."

He nods.

"You'll have to come over and give me and Tom driving lessons sometime. And make sure you don't go dying on me until you teach me the four-up," Bob says, and the old man raises his cane in acknowledgment and hobbles over to his truck.

"He has the best memory," Bob says, as we drive north from the café. "Forrest called me one night and did his foreman thing, asked what I had planned for the next few days, because he needed me to drive him to eastern Washington for a draft horse show he was judging. The entire drive, he'd point out ranches and tell stories about them. One place was owned by a couple who had two boys. The parents didn't want them to leave the ranch and move to the city when they grew up, so they had the boys castrated. Can you imagine?"

I shake my head.

"It worked, I guess. Forrest said one of the brothers was the indoor man, did all the books and management, and the other was the outside man. I asked him, 'Did they both have big barrel chests and high voices?' He asked me how I knew."

"Like eunuchs?"

"Yeah," Bob says. "You know, I once heard a recording of Moreschi, the last of the castrati. His voice was four times more powerful than any tenor living today."

I pull behind Bob's rig and park my truck. Big red letters painted on the trailer's back door spell out:

CAUTION
HORSES TRAINED
TO AIM AT
TAILGATERS

"Let's jump in my truck," he says.

I remember the first time I saw Bob, just down the highway at the bar on that September night. "My father-in-law and I heard you singing karaoke once."

"That must have been a while ago," he says, starting his truck. "I don't get out much anymore."

"Two, two and a half years ago," I say. "I can't remember what song it was."

"Probably 'Unchained Melody.' I only know two songs." He turns off the highway onto the narrow lane. "I came out here from Sacramento to attend Montana State. After I graduated, I got a job teaching music in Flaxville."

"Never heard of it," I say.

"It's up in the northeast corner of the state, near Alberta and North Dakota. You know what they grow in Flaxville?"

"I don't know. Flax?"

"No, pot. But that's another story. After teaching there for a year I got accepted into the conservatory in Cincinnati and sang professionally for the next fifteen or so years." He stops the truck in front of the house. "Now I sing to my horses. They seem to like Puccini. 'Ch'ella mi creda libero' from *The Girl of the Golden West.*"

We get out of the truck. At the slamming doors, the colt picks his head up. He's still tied to the swather. "There he is," I say.

"If I'd known he was tied like that," Bob says rigidly, "I'd have got him right away."

As we get closer, I can see that the lead rope is hung up on the rusty metal cover of the swather. There is a small scrape on the horse's chest. I feel responsible. I am responsible. I have to start acting like I actually own this animal.

Bob gets another rope from his truck, walks up to the horse, and hooks the new lead to the halter, stroking the horse's neck. He unsnaps the rope that's hung up and lays the loose end on the swather. I open the back door to the trailer and Bob leads the colt in, ties him up, and we are done. No problem.

On the way down the potholed lane, back to the turnout where my truck is parked, Bob says, "I'm going to have to bite my tongue next time I see those guys."

"It's my fault," I admit. "I should have known better. I should have called and asked them to take the horse down to the corral once I knew we were stopping for lunch."

"Doesn't matter," Bob says. "Ten minutes would have been too much to leave a horse tied up that way."

We stop at the turnout on the highway and I jump in my truck. I follow Bob, watching the colt's nose poke through the slats of the stock trailer. He is out in the larger world now, moving. We drive west, around the lake, then north through town, and across the bridge spanning the place where the lake empties into the lower Flathead River. Bob pulls into the gravel parking lot of his store and parks. I roll my window down and he says, "I need to come back here when we're done, so why don't you just jump in with me?" I park my truck next to the wagons advertising FORREST DAVIS FREIGHT COMPANY.

We listen to old cowboy songs on the tape player as Bob drives. Don Cadden's "Lil' Ol' Wall-eyed Bay," "Sadie the Mule," and "Roundup in the Spring." We fly north, up the long stretch of Sunny Slope Hill, around the west side of the lake, past Wild Horse Island, the largest of the lake's twenty-two islands. We drive through the tiny community of Big Arm, named for the appendage of water stretching inland from the main body of the lake. Up and over the hill, toward Elmo, where the low ridge of hills that runs west to east, part of the Salish Range, ends abruptly, just before it meets the lake. The face of the last mountain is called Chief Cliff, which drops a hundred and fifty feet to the valley floor.

Bob turns off the highway and drives down a gravel road through the timbered hillside. The lane bends back to the north and we drive under the outstretched limbs of ponderosa pines. We pass a low-slung house with red siding, a trampoline in the yard. Bob stops in front of a green metal gate and I get out to open it. Here the gravel changes to dirt. Once through, we drive down the dirt road for a few hundred yards and finally come out of the timber to an open flat of grass. To the right, there are corrals and a large rectangular arena. Next to the arena, there is a tall red building the size of a two-story phone booth. Its copper roof catches the afternoon sun. To the left stands a huge barn sided in red sheet metal. Three cupolas perch atop the roof. A big white overhead door at one end of the barn faces us. There are pieces of horse-drawn machinery—an old road grader, a wagon, and what looks like a little red chariot—lined up neatly along the fence. A yellow bulldozer is parked like a huge flower in the grass beyond the barn. There are no junked cars, nothing dangerous for the colt to get hung up on. The lake shimmers in the distance. It is more beautiful than I could have imagined.

"Here we are," Bob says. "I'll get the door for you." He parks the truck and grabs the baggie with the vaccinations. I open the rear gate on the trailer, talking softly to the colt, unsure of his reaction to being hauled down the highway at sixty miles an hour. I carefully untie the lead rope and turn him around inside the trailer. We move slowly, both taking a cautious step down onto solid ground. Bob has thrown open the big white overhead door on the barn and he waves us in. I lead the horse past a little red manure spreader, then past a framework of steel painted black and draped in ropes and chains. We step through the open door, the colt's hooves echoing on the concrete floor.

Inside, there are two enclosed stalls on the right, each ten feet by twenty feet, then beyond, three open stalls, two of which are filled with tools and tack. We stop in the middle of the barn. Bob holds the colt's rope while I get the vaccinations ready. First the five-way. With the needle and plastic hub in my right hand, I punch the colt's neck lightly, once, twice, three times. And on the fourth, I jab the needle into his neck. He doesn't react. I inject the vaccine, then do the same with the West Nile shot. Finally, I take out the tube of wormer paste and study the plastic dosage dial that you set according to the horse's weight. I look at Bob. "What do you think?"

"Give him the whole thing," he laughs. "He's wormier than hell."

I stick the tube alongside the colt's teeth as far as I can, then shoot the paste into the back of his mouth. He swallows it reluctantly, working his tongue back and forth. Bob leads the colt to the second stall, ties the rope to a ring screwed into the wall, then he puts a flake of hay in the feeder.

"This is my barn," Bob says, throwing his hands out. "It's a work in progress. This, over here," he points to a framed-in room, "is going to be my office. Someday we'll have a little refrigerator for medicine, a stereo, and a computer. And alongside of that," he points to open concrete, "we'll have a tack room. When we get finished, I'm going to move all of that stuff up on top." He motions toward an air hockey table, a skee-ball game, and a foosball table against the far wall of the barn. "Then we'll build a railing along the top, so none of my kids fall off." Three go-carts are parked in a row near the door at the opposite end of the barn. "That's what happens when you get divorced," Bob explains. "You get dad guilt and overcompensate by buying your kids lots of toys."

Bob points at a little pile of scrap lumber stacked neatly along the wall of the office, the ends of a few two-by-fours, and there is a plastic cup containing three nails. "My carpenter, Fred, is so tickled that he can build something big like this and have so little left over," Bob says. "Let me show you my stud horse."

He walks over to the other stall and flips a light switch. The fluorescent light flickers then pops on. I peer in. The horse has a dark, honey-colored hide and a white-blond tail and mane which he tosses impatiently. The muscles under his hide remind me of the waves on the lake, shimmering in the light. This horse is huge. He fills the entire stall. Compared with my little colt, this stallion looks like a bleached blond, muscle-bound weightlifter.

"What's his name?"

"Schlosstein. I call him Schloss for short. He was the top stud colt in Germany last year. He's just two."

This huge horse is younger than my little colt.

"I'm planning to cross Oberlanders with other breeds to produce larger saddle horses with gentle dispositions," Bob says. He knocks on a board across the opening alongside the stall door. "I had to put this up because he's been trying to break out." Bob runs his hand along the board. "I used cottonwood for all of the stalls, because it's not supposed to splinter. Let's keep your colt in a stall for a while, so we can feed him some grain and get him to gain weight. We should deal with those hooves, too. Do you know how to shoe?"

I shake my head.

"Well, there's no time to learn like the present."

Bob gathers his shoeing tools—the hoof knife, nippers, and rasp—and puts on a pair of short leather chaps. In the stall, I hold the lead rope while Bob starts cleaning the sole of the colt's hoof with the knife. "You want to get right down to that white," he explains, scraping at the old dirt and manure. He carves a channel along the hoof wall, to guide his nippers, then clips the overgrown hoof evenly.

"See these ridges?" Bob asks, pointing at irregular lines across the front of the colt's hoof. "Looks like he might have founder." He works in silence for a while, then says, "And here's a sand crack we're going to need to watch."

I never thought to look at the colt's hooves before I bought him. There is a saying, "No foot, no horse." Founder can occur when a horse gets too much rich feed, or when it drinks too much water when it's been overworked. A foundered horse's feet can become inflamed, resulting in tissue damage, and often a telltale ridge forms in the horse's hooves. A sand crack isn't nearly as serious, but it can still be a problem. It's a tiny fissure in the hoof wall which, if left untreated, can become a larger crack.

"Well," Bob says, "I just filed a little notch perpendicular to the crack. We'll just have to keep an eye on him." When he is done trimming the front hooves, Bob turns his back and holds the colt's right rear hoof between his legs. He says, "I would have thought he'd put up more of a fight. Watch, though, this is when he'll kick me in the nuts."

But no, the colt barely moves, and I am grateful for his manners. I stroke his neck while Bob finishes the last hoof.

"He might get a little friskier once he gets over his worms," Bob says, straightening up and putting his tools away in a little metal tray. "But right now, he's my favorite horse of the day." Bob unbuckles his chaps and says, "Forrest will point out a bay and say, 'That horse is my favorite color.' Then he'll see a gray or a sorrel and say the same thing. I finally called him on it. I asked him how all these different horses could be his favorite color." Bob hangs his chaps on a nail in the next stall.

"What'd he say?"

"He said, 'My favorite color is gentle.'" Bob pats my colt on the neck and says, "You can trim overgrown hooves and you can put weight on a thin horse, but you can't change a horse's disposition."

The colt looks ragged under the barn's fluorescent lights. His dark brown hair is falling off in clumps. But he's gotten vaccinated and his hooves are trimmed and he is in a good place.

There is a light blue recliner outside the stall with a big plastic garbage can next to it. Bob lifts the lid and fills the coffee can inside with molasses-soaked grain. He dumps it in the feed dish in the colt's stall. "We'll give him half a can in the morning and the same again at night," Bob says. "Plus ten pounds of hay each feeding. He'll look like a horse in no time."

The colt drops his head to the sawdust and snorts, then lifts it and begins munching hay. We stand, watching him eat.

"Yep," Bob says, "I think he's a good one."

One Good Horse

The trail boss of a big Wyoming outfit winters in Lincoln because he has a girl there. He hires nineteen-year-old Teddy and four other cowboys to ride over the mountains to Oregon and bring the cattle back to the ranch in Cheyenne. For Teddy, it's a chance to head farther north and west than he has ever gone before. Just as he is ready to say his good-byes, Teddy runs into a cowboy who made the same trip the previous year. "Rained for three weeks straight," he tells Teddy, "and I ain't dry yet." Teddy imagines living outside, cold and soaked through, thinking you'll never be warm or dry again. He decides to head south instead.

He joins up with a young man he knows from back in Lincoln, and soon they find themselves in the tiny parched town of Conejos, in the San Luis Valley of Colorado, just a mile north of the border with New Mexico. It is the end of the line for the train that runs south from Denver. His friend, originally from North Adams, Massachusetts, can't stomach the alkaline water, the heat, the sand, the sage, the Mexicans. It's all too much for him, and after a week, they shake hands and part ways.

Teddy's got his saddle and his war bag packed with clothes. He rides the hat-tipping sorrel. He is hungry and hot. Too much sun and never enough water. He feels his insides going dry. In the saloon he recognizes Bill Charlton, a man he knows from back home. Charlton is tall and dark, a gambler willing to bet on cards or dice, cattle or horses.

He is going to New Mexico to take possession of a herd of seven hundred horses, then trail them back to his ranch at Saltillo, fifteen miles south of Lincoln. He hires Teddy to help.

They ride three hundred miles south, to the Rio Grande, where the herd grazes, guarded by four Mexicans. The horses are gaunt and hollow-eyed. Raised in Texas, stolen south, then back again. They are tired of men running them from one place to another, so many crossings through the river. Charlton counts out twenty-one hundred dollars in gold coins, three dollars a head, and divides it among the four Mexicans. They rest along the banks of the big river for ten days, letting the horses gain strength for the twelve-hundred-mile journey ahead.

Charlton and Teddy, two other cowboys, and a Mexican make the trip. The Mexican is short and dark-skinned. He rides the rankest of the horses first and will not be thrown. After the worst in the bunch rears over backward with the Mexican still clinging to the saddle, the man smiles, nods, and says, "Very good, these one."

Charlton is too tall to be a good rider. A big cold-backed blue roan gives him trouble, dropping his head and bucking a little. Charlton jerks the reins sharply, plants his big Mexican spurs into the horse's flanks, and yells, "Go on, you devil." The horse pitches wildly and Charlton shouts, "Whoa, Blue!" But the horse can feel the rider's weight unbalanced on his back. He bucks one more time and Charlton is thrown from the saddle. As he falls, the cinch hook above the rowels of one of his spurs gets hung up on the rigging of the saddle. The big roan takes off running, dragging Charlton through the cactus and sage, hundreds of miles between him and home.

The horse Teddy rides is rank as well, but he manages to race up alongside the big blue roan. He can hear Charlton's body thudding across the hardpan soil. Reaching, Teddy grabs the cheekstrap of Charlton's headstall and, as he dives out of the saddle, his own spur gets caught on the cantle. He feels something give in his arm. Caught between the two horses, Teddy finally drops to the ground, still holding Charlton's bridle. He turns the horse in a tight circle, managing to loosen Charlton's cinch. The saddle and the man fall to the ground in a heap. Charlton curses the horse and horses, Mexico and Mexicans. But he knows he is lucky to be alive. He looks over at Teddy, who is holding his damaged arm, and asks, "What have I got you want?"

Teddy remembers a sawed-off bay the Mexican was riding a week ago. The little horse wasn't the best in the bunch, not particularly young or handsome, but the way he started from a dead stop, the way he ran as if his tail was on fire, caught Teddy's eye. "Give me that little bay horse," he says.

Charlton shakes his head, wanting to give Teddy something more, something better. "Hell, take a good horse."

But the bay is what Teddy wants.

The life of a man, saved.

What have I got you want?

One good horse.

Chapter Three

IN WARNER VALLEY, THE GREAT HORSES RAN
THE HARD, DRY HAY FIELDS IN THE SUMMER
BEFORE DAYBREAK, THEIR HOOVES ECHOING
ON SOD AS I HERDED THEM THROUGH MISTS
TOWARD THE WILLOW-WALLED CORRAL AT
SOME HAY CAMP. I COULD SEE MYSELF IN
THOSE MASSIVE CREATURES. IF THEY LOVED
THIS WORLD AS THEY SEEMED TO, ON THOSE
MORNINGS WHEN OUR BREATH FOGGED
BEFORE US, THEN SO DID I.

—WILLIAM KITTREDGE,
The Nature of Generosity

The colt rolls in the fresh sawdust, the smell filling his head. He tucks his legs under his body, stands, and shakes. There is no breeze to drift the dust as it rises from his hide and settles along his back and his mane and the floor of the stall. He steps to the opening adjacent to the stall door and sniffs. In the next stall, the big draft stud tilts his head sideways, to reach through the gap between the stall and the board that has been nailed over the opening, and he nips the colt's muzzle, then squeals and kicks the wall behind him.

The colt retreats. He has never been in an enclosed building in his entire life. No wind. No sun or moon or stars. The sound of a mouse running. The talons of a bird scratching the metal roof above, echoing against the concrete floor.

And now the little door to the barn opens. The stallion nickers. But this is not the man who feeds them in the morning. This man pulls on the rope that opens the big overhead door and daylight floods the barn. It is almost like being outside now, but it isn't. The man backs a blue pickup into the barn, then gets out. He takes a tool belt from the bed of the truck and buckles it around his waist. He measures boards and marks them. The circular saw screams to life, ripping through the board as the man cuts it to length. The smell of sawdust, again. The man hammers the boards into place, framing the door to the office. When the man breaks for lunch, he takes off his tool belt and opens the door to his truck and lays the belt on the front bench. He turns, eyes narrowing, and walks over to the second stall. Surprised to see another animal in the barn, he looks at the skinny brown colt and asks, "Now whose horse are you?"

After the babies wake from their morning nap, Jennifer has Carter put away his schoolwork and we eat lunch. Grilled cheese sandwiches and apple juice and fresh strawberries. Then Jennifer kisses me on the cheek, says, "Drive safe," and she lets me go.

She is giving me this time, this space, to go to the ranch, and I am just selfish enough to take it. The horse is an excuse to get out of the house, to get away from the diapers and the drool, from the sadness of Avery's smiling face. What happened last summer—the boys arriving prematurely and Avery's diagnosis—was no one's fault, but sometimes I think Jennifer feels responsible. The countless trips to the hospital in Missoula, then the endless nights staying up with crying infants, all of it more than we ever expected. Now that our family seems to have made it through in one piece, though, Jennifer gives me this little bit of freedom. I might rationalize the time I'll be spending on the colt by saying that someday the kids will be able to ride him, but I know this horse is just for me. It's my way of regaining the last year.

I drive south, past the colt's old pasture, the grass growing tall and green and wild with the absence of horses. Through the two-stoplight town, past Bob's store, and up the west shore of the lake. At the gravel turnout before Big Arm, a car is pulled over and people are taking photos of Wild Horse Island in the distance. The sky is a paler shade of blue than the mountains.

Three of Bob's Oberlander mares and their foals stand around the little muddy pond at the gate below Bob's house. The foals are silly and awkward, racing around the edge of the water before hiding behind their mothers. Looking at the mares, I can see what the young horses will grow into. These horses are magnificent, larger than life.

I close the gate, drive down the hill, and pull up next to the barn. The big white door is up and there is a blue pickup parked inside. Bob's yellow horse trailer is gone.

Inside the barn, a man measures the doorway of the office. He is older, in his sixties, and he wears a leather tool belt around his slim waist.

"Hello," I say, watching as the man stands and the yellow tape snakes back into itself.

He hangs the tape measure on his belt and extends a hand. "Name's Fred," he says. "That must be your little horse, huh?"

"Yeah," I say, "I just bought him. I'm going to trade Bob some work for the colt's room and board." Fred nods. He picks up a two-by-four and sights down it for straightness. "I'm not much of a carpenter," I admit, "but give a shout if you need a hand with anything."

"You bet," he says, laying the board on top of two sawhorses.

The colt is backed into one corner of the stall. "Hey, Bud," I say, softly, unlatching the door. I am half-expecting the colt to spin and kick me, so I move cautiously. There are marks across his nose and cheeks where his old halter wore away the winter hair. It's not bad, just lost hair, but still it marks him. I drape the cotton rope over the colt's mane and pick up the loose end under his neck. "Hey," I whisper. He doesn't seem concerned, but I don't want to let my guard down and have him smoke me. He lifts his nose to me, and I blow into his nostrils gently. I imagine my breath smells of grilled cheese and apples and nerves. I buckle the halter behind his head and lead him out of the stall, onto the concrete floor toward the overhead door. Fred is facing away from me, leaning over the sawhorse, and I see too late that he is holding a circular saw. The saw comes to life, ripping through the board, the whine of the cut echoing in the metal barn. But the colt just keeps walking beside me.

Maybe, like Bob said, it's the worms that have taken the fight out of him. I tie the colt to a post in one of the small pens alongside the arena, then walk back to the barn to get a curry comb and a brush. I work on brushing out the colt's winter coat for the next fifteen minutes. Clouds of dry brown hair collect in piles at our feet. "Hey, Bud," I say. I comb out the tangled black mane, trying to get it to fall on one side of his neck or the other, but most of it sticks up like a little boy's cowlick. Next I brush out the colt's ratty tail. He doesn't even try to kick me. Instead, he rubs the side of his face on the post. I don't know what else to do. Maybe today's lessons will be grooming and patience. I leave him tied and watch as a pair of ducks wing overhead, flying toward the lake.

In the distance, Wild Horse Island seems to bob like a toy in the huge bathtub of Flathead Lake. At 2,165 acres, or roughly three and a half square miles, it is the largest of the lake's twenty-two islands. Its soil is mostly glacial till, with grasslands to the island's south and timbered hills rising more than a thousand feet to the north. The grass is the last vestige of Montana's native range, the Palouse Prairie, a fragile ecosystem.

According to one version of the story, Wild Horse Island earned its name in the early 1700s, when the Kootenai

Indians gathered a herd of horses and swam them out to the island to hide them from raiding Blackfeet warriors. After the Blackfeet had moved on, the Kootenais rounded up as many of the horses as they could and brought them back to the mainland. A small band of horses remained behind, growing wild, the island their new home. Now there are about fifty private homes on the island, but the balance of the land is managed as a primitive park by the state of Montana. Three mustangs still run free on the island as a nod to the past.

I walk back to the barn to clean the stalls.

"Make any progress?" Fred asks, when he sees me.

"I don't know," I say. "I've never trained a horse before, so I'm going slow." He nods and goes back to his work. I fill the wheelbarrow with three piles of manure and some urine-soaked sawdust from the colt's stall. The manure is bright green from the alfalfa hay. I don't see any worms in it and, as far as I can tell, it looks healthy. Next I move to the stallion's stall. He bulls right up to me, curious, the white stripe down the center of his nose right in my face. I push him away gently, saying, "Go on, Schloss." But he stands his ground, proud and full of himself. I work around him cautiously, scooping up a couple of piles before slipping out of the stall. I steer the wheelbarrow outside and dump it into the manure spreader.

There is nothing left to do but get the colt and bring him back to the barn. Once I've turned him loose in the stall, I fill the colt's water bucket, feed him a half can of sweet feed and some hay. Before I leave, I walk back to the pen by the arena and pick up the clumps of brown hair and a stray Pop-Tart wrapper. I put the wrapper in my pocket and drop the big brown hair ball in the bed of my truck. I'm not sure why I do it. I guess I'm just trying to pick up after myself. As I accelerate down the highway toward town, tufts of brown hair blow out of the bed of my truck, marking my path from horse to home.

As I near town, I see flashing red and blue lights in front of Three Dog Down. I slow the truck and coast past. In the gravel parking lot of Bob's store, two police cars and a large motor home have pulled off the highway. A banner on the RV reads: TORCH RUN, SPECIAL OLYMPICS. And it hits me again. All of the things that will never be. In front of the Lake City Bakery, people stand on the sidewalk, waiting. Farther on, in front of the bank, more people. I ghost past in my white pickup, not any kind of hero worth cheering for.

Sometimes I forget that everything is going to be okay.

April 23, 1904. The United States Congress passes a bill which declares that all reservation lands should be surveyed in anticipation of settlement by whites. Indians are allotted parcels ranging from eighty to one hundred sixty acres, depending on the desirability of the land. Though the reservation boundary line cuts Flathead Lake in two running east to west, all of the lake's islands are given to the Tribe. After the new bill is signed, small villa lots of two to five acres are formed on the islands. These villa sites are available to Flathead tribal members as allotments, but only a handful are claimed. The remaining lots go to homesteaders. A number of families make the barge trip out to Wild Horse Island with a cow or two, a plow, some building supplies.

Nine years pass. The U.S. government auctions off more lots on the reservation. Colonel Almond A. White, a land speculator who hails from St. Paul, purchases more than half of these new lots, paying fifteen dollars an acre for most of the interior land on the island, and up to fifty dollars an acre for the villa sites along the shore. White is convinced he can double his money once his plans to develop the island are realized.

White hires two men to guide tourists visiting Glacier National Park south to Flathead Lake in a seven-passenger automobile. As they drive, the guides expound upon the wonders of Wild Horse Island. *Sure, Glacier Park is beautiful, they say, but how would you like to own a piece of land in a place just as beautiful, no, even more beautiful?*

At the docks, they meet the colonel. He wears a dapper cream-colored suit with a handkerchief in his breast pocket. The prospective buyers board a narrow white skiff named the *Helen R* and they sit, wide-eyed, as they listen to the colonel's plans for Wild Horse Island. White points out where the fourteen miles of roads will soon go. He promises twenty miles of bridle paths. An observatory will be built up on Lakota Peak, just like the Lick Observatory in California. The skiff bobs around to the northeast side of the island. The Montana sun doubled again and again in tiny water mirrors. There will be a power plant. A hotel. An indoor swimming pool. *The Natatorium,*

White calls it. Two ferries will make a circuit around the lake, each with the capacity to carry a thousand passengers and thirty automobiles. *Can you imagine?* The golf course, the yacht club. Colonel White sits in the stern, his hand on the rudder, steering the conversation this way and that, homing in on the closing. The tourists are impressed. They get off on the mainland, shake the colonel's hand, and promise to be in touch.

But no one calls.

Bob phones. "I wanted to let you know that I didn't see any piles in your colt's stall when I went down to the barn tonight."

"There were three big ones that I cleaned up," I say.

"Oh, well that's good," he says. "I hope it's okay with you, but I needed to move your horse to one of the pens outside. I brought Leroy and his mother home from the vet's and I put them in the stall in the barn because I want to keep them from moving around too much."

"Leroy?"

"Yeah," he says. "I named the foal after the vet so that he'll take extra special care of his namesake."

"What's wrong with him?"

"Well, he's a workaholic and he can't carry a tune to save his life, but other than that—"

"No," I laugh, "what's wrong with the foal?"

"The X-rays showed a fractured stifle. We're not sure how it happened. Hopefully, he'll get better. If he doesn't, well, we just have to wait and see."

As he waits, he remembers.

That past year a blur of sickness, whiskey, dust. He quit Bill Charlton's outfit in Colorado, the bay horse the only good thing to come of it. He named the horse Little Billy, in honor of Charlton. Then the mountain fever took hold in LaVeta, that tiny town snug up against the Sangre de Cristo Mountains. Days and nights of shivering and weakness, his stomach turning inside out, his muscles so sore he could hardly walk. The sun too bright.

When he felt well enough, he bailed Little Billy out of the livery stable. It was good being back in the open air, on the back of a solid horse. They drifted south, to the Pecos, where he hired on with John Chisum's Jingle Bob outfit. And it was a fine job, until that blue-eyed, goofy-grinned kid started trouble. Bill Antrim or Will McCarty or Bill Bonney or whatever he called himself. The Kid could sing like a grimy, bucktoothed angel, his falsetto voice setting off the coyotes, the Spanish lyrics floating out across the arid New Mexico scrub. The Kid claimed Chisum owed him five hundred dollars, and that he'd shoot one hired man for every fifty dollars of what he was owed. He said he'd already shot three, blood washing away part of the debt. But there was three hundred and fifty dollars—or seven men—left. Teddy watched his back constantly, and that wasn't any way to live, looking over his shoulder. So, after the last of the cattle were branded, he drew his wages and rode east, cussing Billy the Kid with each dry, lonely mile.

He remembers El Paso, down in the far corner of Texas, along the border with Mexico, old and new. The Pass. That town, with the railroad coming in, was wild. Sin City, they called it. The random gunfire and the fire in his gut from all that poor whiskey. Mexicans, outlaws from across the river, lying dead in the street. He had no part in it but he was there when they turned one of the bodies over. It was a woman dressed as a man. Just a girl, bleeding from the chest. An old Texas gunslinger once said, "You always want to shoot 'em in the right eye because that disturbs their aim." He thought it was funny at the time, they all did, but this was different.

Right after, he found a herd of longhorns going north and he left that town behind. So many cattle flowing north, like a big, bawling, rusty river, their horns catching the same sun over Texas, the Indian Nations, Kansas, and Nebraska. Once they made Ogallala, the cattle were bought by old John Blocker, the man who sold his father his first steers so many years ago. The trail had brought him home.

He waits. In a month, he'll be twenty-one. He's spent the better part of a year trying to talk his father into giving him the three thousand dollars left to him by one of his uncles, one of his father's wealthy solicitor brothers. It's enough to buy that little place in Colorado, the one with the box canyon and the stream. He wouldn't need to build much fence, just some across the mouth of the canyon. The rock walls would hold the cattle and shelter them from the weather. He could make a start there.

But his father isn't hearing any of it, like his ears are

packed with dirt. His father telling him, "You are a wastrel." His father telling him he'll just spend the money on cheap women and expensive horses. Telling him he'll drink it all up and piss it away by the time he's twenty-five. His father telling him he should give up being a cow-puncher and become a farmer.

The months of waiting finally pass, and when he turns twenty-one, he gets his money. But instead of heading off to Colorado, he stays. He buys a little herd of cattle, making good on part of his plan. And then he gets sick again. Lung fever. Days spent laid out in the cold bed, coughing, coughing. He coughs so hard that he spits up something hard and metallic. A bullet. It happened a year and a half ago, but he can't remember who shot him, or why.

Once the bullet is out, he feels better. So good, in fact, that he starts drinking. But that's not so much the problem as the fact that he's still living under his father's roof. It's like he's a ten-year-old kid again. He knows he has to go.

It's Saturday morning, the first of May. Avery and Bennett sit in their high chairs in the kitchen and Jennifer feeds them scrambled eggs and slices of banana. Carter watches Saturday morning cartoons. The phone rings and it's Bob. "Forrest is coming out sometime after noon to help me trim the stallion," he says. It sounds like he is eating something, a Pop-Tart maybe. "You should come out, if you can."

"Sounds good," I say. "I'll be there."

But I am reluctant to go. I remember Bob telling me

that Forrest doesn't spare anyone's feelings, that he doesn't have time to gentle his opinions. I'm afraid that once the old man gets a look at my colt, he will come to the same conclusion he did with the horses he hauled to the animal sanctuary. *Can 'em.*

I pull down the driveway to Bob's place. Forrest's white Chevy is parked in front of the house, and they are just heading down to the barn in the Gator, a six-wheeled John Deere that looks like a big green golf cart. Bob waves and I follow in my pickup, closing gates behind us as we go.

I park at the barn. Bob is in the stallion's stall, haltering the big horse. Forrest stands outside the second stall, peering in at Leroy. Forrest wears a long-sleeved maroon work shirt over thermal underwear. He's got the same Wrangler jeans that have been let out at the waist, the wooden cane, the suspenders. He wears a white straw cowboy hat with black ribbon bound into the brim.

"Mr. Tom," Bob calls out as he exits the stud's stall. "How the heck are you?"

"Good," I say. "Nice day."

"That it is," Bob says. "That it is."

Forrest walks past, looks up, and nods at me as he enters the stallion's stall. The little old man hooks his cane over his arm and reaches up to redo the knot on the halter. The horse towers over him. "Now what's that look like?" he asks Bob.

"Looks like a real knot," Bob says, noting the correction. Bob bends down and tries to pick up one of the horse's huge hooves, but he can barely lift it off the ground.

"Get some rope," Forrest says. The old man ties a loop in the rope that Bob hands him, then he runs the loose end through the loop and puts it around the stallion's left rear foot. Forrest pulls on the rope with both hands, testing the give of the hoof. The stud's foot doesn't budge. The old man runs the end of the rope around the stallion's neck and back down to the hoof again and ties a slipknot. This arrangement doesn't choke the horse, but it lets him feel the weight of his own leg. Eventually he'll learn to pick his hoof up, to take the pressure off his neck.

"What's the hardest you've ever been kicked, Forrest?" Bob asks. "By a horse, I mean."

"Well, one time I got kicked square in the face." Forrest reaches up to his face and makes a motion. "Had to move my nose away from my eye." He relates the story like it's shoptalk, like it's no big deal. The stallion has stopped struggling now and he holds his hoof off the ground. Forrest motions to the horse. "Go ahead, untie him and pick it up."

Bob looks a little unsure, but does what he is told. He struggles to pick up the huge hoof, managing to lift it a few inches off the ground.

"Tie him up again if he is going to piss around," Forrest says. "Give him twenty minutes. We'll go look at that colt, if that's what we're gonna do."

My colt stands in the pen alongside the arena. Compared with Bob's stallion, he looks like a skinny, sad mistake. I unlatch the gate and close it behind me. I hope the colt doesn't give me any problems, pray he doesn't make me look bad in front of Forrest. I approach him with the halter and rope, talking to him softly, saying, "Hey, boy." He trots to the far corner of the pen and stands with his rear toward me. It's not a good sign, his showing me his rump, as if he is warning me that he'll kick me if I don't back off. I move up to him slowly, watching his hooves and his ears for any signs that he is going to strike. I reach out and stroke his neck. He flinches, but lets me halter him without a fight, then I lead him over to a post and tie him there.

Forrest hooks his cane over the top rail of the pen and stands outside as I brush the colt. "Bob says he was hung up when you went to load him."

"Yes," I say. "He was tied to an old piece of junk."

"Is there anything over there but junk?"

"It was a Hesston swather," I say. "I should have known better."

He lets this pass. "They still have a corral made out of old cars?"

"No," I say, picturing a circle of junked vehicles, the gate to the corral a car door. "I saw a lot of old cars, but they weren't a corral."

Forrest watches the colt. "That guy used to have quite a few horses over there, but he had a sale a few years back. Sold a hundred head or so after he lost some leases." Forrest unlatches the gate and walks into the little pen. "He's got a Thoroughbred front and a quarter horse rear," he says, running his hand over the colt's hind end and then down one leg. "Which isn't good or bad, it's just the way he is. He's got a nice gaskin. That's from the quarter horse."

I stand against the rails of the pen, bracing myself for

Forrest's final judgment, for him to say, *If this horse was mine, I'd can him.* I don't know why it matters so much to me, what this man thinks.

He moves to the front of the horse and reaches up and unties the lead rope. He holds the end of the rope in one hand and looks in the colt's mouth with the other. "He's two, two and a half. That's what his teeth tell me."

Bob is here now, leaning over the rail. "Do that thing with the eye," he says.

Forrest reaches up and pushes on the loose skin under the colt's eyelid, making a wrinkle. "Well, he has one wrinkle, which means he's two. Each wrinkle means a different age. A twelve-year-old will have four wrinkles."

"And would you call him long- or short-backed?" Bob asks.

"Long-backed. From here, at the withers," Forrest gestures, "to the here, at the point of the hip. A long-backed horse will have a little smoother gait, but he'll have more problems carrying the weight. I prefer a short-backed horse."

"I wanted you to take a look at his hooves," Bob says. "Is that founder?"

Forrest bends over and studies the ridges in the colt's hooves. "No, that's not founder," he says. He points at a spot on the hoof. "That's just where he was without food for a while." He points at another spot. "And then here he got into too much grain. It's nothing serious."

He straightens up and hands me the rope and says, "He's a nice colt, Tom."

That's it. *He's a nice colt.* Forrest has seen thousands of horses in his lifetime, the good ones and the bad. I'm certain that, beyond the shedding hair and the protruding ribs, the colt must have his faults, yet Forrest has chosen to give him a passing grade. And more than that, what feels good is that Forrest remembered my name. *He's a nice colt, Tom.*

Back in the barn, the stud has come around enough to let Bob pick up each of his massive hooves.

"Good enough," Forrest says. "Let's get him trimmed."

Bob leads the horse from its stall and into the black metal contraption just outside the barn door. Ropes and chains covered in old fire hose hang from the framework of steel. "Forrest's son-in-law builds these," Bob explains. "It's a shoeing stock." Bob leads the horse up to the stanchion, but the horse balks. Forrest lifts his wooden cane and taps the stallion's rear, coaxing it forward. The horse steps up and Bob ties the lead rope. He fastens a chain behind the stallion's tail, then he secures two chains across the stallion's back, to keep him from rearing up. Bob picks up the horse's right front leg and positions it in a metal support, then lashes it down with a soft rope. All of this, just so he can trim the horse's hoof safely.

As Bob works with the nippers and rasp, Forrest interrupts from time to time. "Take more off there," he says, "it's still uneven."

When the first hoof is done, Bob unties the rope and the stallion lifts his leg and stands on it. The leg shakes spastically. "Oh, they all do that," Forrest says, his own oversized blue-veined hands quivering at his sides, ever so slightly. He moves behind the horse, looking at its tail. "Rat's nest."

Bob looks like a little boy in trouble. "Uh, that just happened yesterday."

Forrest clears his throat. He doesn't believe it.

"Maybe it's been a week," Bob says.

"More like since you got him," Forrest scolds. "You got a good comb or a knife?"

While Bob retrieves a knife, Forrest leans on the stanchion and removes his left shoe, a leather slip-on, and dumps a stone out of it. He wears dark blue dress socks. Bob returns, hands Forrest a knife, and the old man starts running the blade between the strands of hair to untangle them. He is a small man, but his hands are huge from a lifetime of labor.

Bob resumes his work on the stallion's hooves. "So you're telling me that tail wouldn't pass muster in the army?" He smiles and winks at me.

Forrest snorts.

"I, for one, would like to thank you for your service," Bob says. "Tell Tom what you did for the army."

"Broke horses at Fort Sill," Forrest says.

"He's the only soldier in the history of the United States military to never learn how to salute or make his bed," Bob says. "He was too busy breaking horses. Then they sent him to Normandy for D-Day."

"I was in the sixth wave," Forrest says. "There were one hundred and twenty-five men in my unit. They sent us over on the *Queen Mary*. It took four days to get there.

And when we were done doing what we had to do, they weren't in any rush to get us back. The return trip took eighteen days, and there were only twenty-three of us left."

I watch the men work, Forrest untangling the stallion's knotted tail, Bob sweating over the hooves. He cleans each with a hoof pick, uses the nippers to trim them, then files them even with a rasp. When he's done, Bob packs his shoeing tools in the little metal tray and takes them back to the barn. Forrest unfastens the chains, unties the stallion's lead rope, and hands it to me. "We've pissed around with him long enough," he says. "Take him back to his stall."

I don't really feel like I can handle the stallion, but I do what I am told. It's like holding on to a tiger's tail, this horse so different from the little colt I ended up with. I lead the stallion back to his stall, trotting alongside the massive horse to keep up with him.

Bob watches from the front door of the office, sipping from a bottle of water. Forrest hobbles into the barn and sits in the sky blue recliner. "Have some water, Forrest," Bob says, walking over with another bottle. But Forrest waves him off and closes his eyes, falling asleep to the smell of sawdust and leather and manure and horses.

Colonel White's dreams for Wild Horse Island are unraveling. It's taking too long. He is behind on his payments. In 1923, the colonel forfeits most of the lots to the government for back taxes, and he takes a loss on the rest.

Two years later, Reverend Robert Edgington, a retired pastor from New York, purchases a number of lots at auction for fifty dollars each, buying a total of forty acres. Edgington, who lives in nearby Dayton, builds a large lodge on a deepwater cove on the island's east side. He runs the place as a dude ranch, using his connections back east to bring people to the ranch. The place is named Hiawatha Lodge, a nod to Longfellow's idyllic poem of native life.

The reverend guides horseback trips; his wife, Clara, runs the lodge. They are making a go of it, sharing the glories of Montana with people from back east, and making money as a result. But then, on an October day in 1934, the weather turns too calm. The wind doesn't even whisper a warning. The sun suddenly obscured by a bank of clouds. The storm hits like a wet, windy fist. Waves crash ashore and trees snap like sticks. Edgington and his hired hand run down to the docks to secure the boats, which splinter as they smash into each other. Edgington's cowboy hat flies into the air and disappears. A wave, a great green watery hand, pulls the men into the lake. The hired man struggles ashore, but Edgington is lost. Clara is shattered, uprooted, set adrift. She packs her things and leaves.

Lewis Penwell, a sheep rancher from Helena, Montana, buys the property from Reverend Edgington's widow in 1938. Penwell tries to make a go of the dude ranch, but he doesn't have the right contacts back east and the resort languishes. Penwell is more interested in turning the island into a refuge for wildlife, rather than a sanctuary for dudes. The island, with its craggy cliffs and grassy flats, is perfect bighorn sheep habitat. In 1939, two bighorn sheep are transplanted, and a year later fifteen mule deer are brought to the island. Penwell also turns his attention to the horses on the island, a handful of castaways descended from the early homesteaders' and Edgington's saddle stock. He purchases a palomino stud and turns it loose on his land. It is Penwell's dream to own the entire island and he goes about buying up as much of it as he can. But by 1943, his cash and his dreams are burned out, and he is ready to move on.

He spends the summer on the North and South Platte Rivers looking over his shoulder. It's not the thought of a bullet from Billy the Kid that scares him, but the damned lightning, a silver, fiery blast from the heavens. In August, one storm killed two men, fourteen cows, and seven horses. One man threw his gun away, thinking the metal might attract a bolt of lightning. Teddy is glad that he spit that bullet out from deep inside. Tiny blue sparks gather in the air. He worries about Little Billy. There is nowhere to take cover on these open plains, lightning falling all around. After that Texas cowboy, Pap, got thrown and trampled that night on the Blue, Teddy sings when he is on night watch, so the others will know where he is. And he sings to the horse now, tunes with words that reassure both of them, about how they will go north someday, to the Yellowstone. Montana Territory, that wild, wide open land. Grass up to your stirrups. No farmers. It's the one place all cowboys long to go.

But that fall, he returns home. The deadeye stare of winter. Too much, too much. Women he can't even remember. Sometimes he can recall the clothes they wore, but nothing else. Whiskey, rivers of it, drowning each amber night. His father was right. He is a wastrel, pissing away his money and his life. And his own cattle have suffered.

When spring finally comes, he sells his small herd and takes the loss and moves on. He kisses his mother good-bye and saddles up Little Billy and rides south. It's April 10, 1883, just outside San Antonio, and he hires on with the FUF, a ranch owned by a businessman from Vermont. Teddy should have known what sort of outfit it was by the people hired to take the cattle north: the kid from Boston with the high-topped brogans which make him look like he is headed for the opera, Biggs the tea-drinking Englishman, the fellow from Louisiana who speaks only French. The mess of them. But Teddy is making good wages, seventy-five dollars a month.

The drive begins in the brushy country of south Texas and will end in Montana, if the horses don't kill him first, the knotheads. Half-wild range horses, five or six to a man. The boss figures he'll make some extra money by getting them broke along the way. Teddy picks out five mustangs that aren't too ringy, and he's got Little Billy.

The first night after they cross the Platte, he is on watch with that kid from Boston. Teddy's bad arm aches and he knows it is going to storm. The sky finally breaks open and hailstones rain down. The horses turn their hindquarters toward the hail and will not budge. Teddy yells to the kid to take his saddle off his horse and hold it over his head, and he does the same. A large hailstone smacks Teddy's hand, he drops the reins, and his night horse takes off into the black. Up all night, all the next day. He is used to working with little sleep, but this is bad.

On the other drives, they'd push cattle all day, bed the herd around nine at night, then get dinner. Two men would take the first two-hour shift, making loops around the herd, meeting up, chatting a bit, sharing a smoke. Then they'd head back around the cattle and check the other side. He could usually count on a few hours of sleep. But that's when things are going good, when you aren't spending the night with hailstones denting the saddle over your head, when you aren't chasing down runaway horses.

He pulls night duty again and he can hardly sit in his hailstone-dented saddle. He rubs tobacco juice in his eyes to keep them open. Another storm in the dead of the night, and the cattle from four other herds run together with the FUF bunch. The next day, ten thousand head need to be sorted under the ever-burning Nebraska sun. No corrals, no shade, no sleep. It doesn't matter. The pain means he is alive.

I lie on the narrow bed in Carter's room, unable to sleep. Carter is curled up in our bed with Jennifer, and the babies sleep in their cribs. I am just an overgrown boy sleeping on sheets printed with bears going sledding. On the walls, framed scribbles and finger paintings. The wooden rocking horse in the corner.

In the house I grew up in, my father had a clock on the wall downstairs inscribed with that line from John Donne's

"Meditation XVII," *No man is an island, entire of itself.* I can't get over the feeling, though, that our family has become an island. We've become so isolated, with twin toddlers, and with Avery, and I am afraid that it will only get worse. We are not joiners, not the type of people who attend support groups. It's not fair to Avery, none of it is fair.

I want to be bigger than this. I want to be a hero for my boys and my wife. I want to save people from burning buildings, pull them from wrecked cars. But more often than not, I feel as if I am the one who needs saving.

The tiny bookshelf filled with children's stories. It was just yesterday that this was all mine, and now it is my son's. I have gray hairs in my whiskers, creases at the folds of my eyes. I tell myself I am laying down my life for my family, that my life is no longer my own. I think about the lies we tell ourselves to make it through the day. Stories about who we are, who we were, who we will become.

Just last week, my parents were visiting. It was the first time we'd seen them since last Christmas. On Sunday we decided to celebrate Mother's Day at the little restaurant Jennifer and Carter and I usually go to. It's a place in the mountains, across from Glacier Park, where the railroad tracks run close by. The walls of the inn are hung with historic photos of steam engines. Outside, helper engines idle, waiting to push freight trains up and over the pass. It was a long drive with all of us crammed in the car. When we got there, the restaurant looked so much smaller than I remembered it. A busboy and a waitress had to push two tables together to accommodate our group. It seemed to me that the other diners finished their meals quickly, looking to get away from the controlled food fight that occurs every time Avery and Bennett eat solids. We had become "those people." Our family has changed in this last year, and I don't always recognize it.

They make Fort Kearny, Nebraska, by the middle of summer. Teddy and three others are sent down to Kansas to bring back another six hundred head. It's two hundred miles, and there's just the four of them with a horse apiece and the lone wagon. Thankfully, he has Little Billy.

Teddy looks out across the land. The whole state of Kansas has turned to farming, it seems. Crops scratched into the soil, ragged fence built around the fields. Nothing substantial enough to keep out a hungry cow, though. The ripening wheat is a foot high and it rattles gold in the July breeze.

For the last ten years, cattle always came through this country. Always. Now the cows are running wild through the wheat and word has reached Teddy and the others that the sheriff is on his way. Everyone wanting his share. After paying out all of the money they were given to cover damages, the cowboys have already had to sell three cows. The corn-fed farmers shake their fists and wave shotguns, claiming what isn't theirs in the first place.

There are still a hundred and forty miles left till they reach Fort Kearny, the land stretching to the horizon painted gold. The horses are played out from running circles around the cattle. The cowboys are beat. Teddy sends word to the boss that the herd will be waiting for them at the next rail yard. They can't move cows like they used to. It can't be done in this changed land.

After they unload the stock cars in Fort Kearny, the boss sends them down to Missouri for more cattle and horses, but this time he's arranged for a train to haul the livestock back. But because he is so miserly, the boss orders the cowboys to bed the first two cars, the ones carrying the horses, with straw instead of sand. When the train pulls a long, low Missouri hill, the engine sends a shower of sparks into the night. Some of the sparks float down into the straw at the feet of the horses. When Teddy sees the flames from the caboose, he runs across the tops of the stock cars, stumbling and reeling in the dark, the fire ahead like a gas lamp, a comet, a shooting star. He fires his gun at the bell on the engine, trying to get the engineer's attention, but it isn't enough. It is too late to save any of them.

A yellow-eyed goat wearing a dirty white coat and stubby horns disappears around the end of the barn when I pull up and park my truck. I get out and follow the goat. He stands next to a black goat on the stack of small square hay bales. They stare at me suspiciously.

In the barn, I can see that Fred the carpenter is making progress. The office now has a door that locks. The tack room is nearly finished. The kids' games have been moved above and there is a railing in place. All of this visible progress contrasts with the invisible steps I've been taking with the colt. And the work I've been doing around the ranch to pay for the colt's board doesn't look like much either. I've cleaned stalls and spread the manure in the fields, but they just get dirty again. I've fixed the barbed wire fence that borders Bob's neighbor to the south, but the wires are loose already. And I've picked rock from the lower pasture until my hands were raw, but for every rock I've hauled to the pile near the barn, a dozen remain in the field.

I push open the office door and turn on the overhead light. There is a mini fridge humming in one corner. A rolltop desk and a chair line the back wall. Tacked at eye level on the walls are a dozen laminated full-color illustrations of the anatomy of a horse. There's an illustration of the ideal conformation of a horse. There are the equine nervous system, the skeleton, a chart of how horse's teeth wear with age. There's illustrations of problems that can happen during birth. It is too much to look at under the clean fluorescent light, all of the things inside a body that can break.

It used to be called mongolism or Mongoloidism, a term which originated with John Langdon Down, the English doctor who, in 1866, first categorized the characteristics of the disorder. He thought people with the condition, with their almond-shaped eyes, looked Asian, thus the name Mongolism. Today, it is known as Down syndrome, in recognition of the doctor's research.

Down syndrome goes to the smallest stuff of life, an extra chromosome in every cell of the body, yet it becomes the biggest fact about a person with the condition. It's what the world sees on the outside of people with Down syndrome, of my son, Avery. A baby, a boy, a man, who consists of symptoms. A laundry list of possible health issues to stare down for the rest of his life: eyesight problems, hearing loss, speech issues, obesity, mental retardation.

When I've been around people with disabilities in the past, I was always at a loss as to how to interact with them. I want to help these people, to give them something, to somehow fix things. But I can't. From the very beginning, I was Avery's protector. I was the one who fed him throughout the night while Jennifer nursed Bennett. But there is a leaden fear, newly born, deep inside of me. I'm afraid, as he gets older, I won't be able to give Avery what he needs.

I remember that day last summer as if it were happening now.

I hold Avery, feeding him a tiny bottle of high-calorie formula. A sleepless night in a strange place. There was the blast of the air conditioner, which I'm not used to, and the sound of a child crying out in pain from down the hall. I got up every two hours to make Avery a bottle and feed it to him. If everything goes right, this is the last time I'll need to visit the hospital. The nurses want to make sure that I know how to give Avery his medicine in the right doses and that I know how to administer oxygen. I learn where to tape the leads to Avery's chest and how to operate the monitor. At five weeks old, he is finally ready to come home.

Avery sucks the bottle down. I should have changed

him before I started feeding him. Sometimes, after eating, Avery throws it all back up. Other times, he stops breathing and his heart rate plunges. These are called apnea/bradycardia spells, a condition that sometimes happens in premature babies. A machine monitors his heart rate, his respiration, and the oxygen level in his blood. When Avery has a spell, the monitor goes off and he needs to be roused. So far he's come out of these spells with a gentle shaking or other stimulation, but when we finally leave this place, we'll be going home with a portable monitor and bottles of oxygen, just in case.

Jennifer and I never could have imagined any of this. We pictured our sons: oldest brother Carter, smart and fast; Avery and Bennett, big, easygoing kids, laughing together. They would carry one another through life's rough patches. But now one of them is missing. Avery, Avery, little star. He was lost from the beginning. Together, our family will have to find Avery, we will have to discover who he is as a person. For now, we put all of this aside and, somehow, keep moving through these gauzy summer days.

Out the window, the haze of forest fires hangs in the early morning light. The room smells faintly of milk gone sour, antiseptic, smoke filtered through the hospital's ventilation system.

I put Avery in my lap, trying to keep him upright while I change his clothes. One of the leads comes loose from his chest, and the monitor beeps loudly, sounding like the alarm on a vehicle backing up. We need to move beyond this. We need to move forward. I punch the button to silence the alarm. I peel the adhesive from Avery's chest and he cries out. There isn't enough room on his tiny chest to position the leads where they are supposed to be, so one goes on sideways, near his armpit. I try to thread the wires through the fresh white outfit Jennifer gave me to bring Avery home in. The wires are so delicate, the clothes so small, and my hands are too large and clumsy. When I've finished, Avery vomits all over everything—his going-home clothes, the blanket in the isolette, me—all baptized in warm formula. He stares at me with watery, deep blue eyes. He is claiming me. For better or worse. I am his. He is mine.

I wipe Avery down as best I can and change him back into the onesie he slept in, then dig around in the diaper bag and find another outfit for him to wear. I push the button to call the nurse. She's got a list of things that need to be done before Avery's discharge. First is the car seat. I need to strap Avery into the seat and watch to make sure he'll be able to travel home without any problems. "If you live an hour and a half away," the nurse says, "we should keep him here that long." It doesn't make any sense to me, but I am not about to argue. There were so many times we got our hopes up in the last five weeks, times we thought the boys would be coming home in a day or two, only to arrive at the hospital and have one of the nurses ask, "Who told you that?" At this point, an hour and a half is nothing.

"In the meantime," the nurse says, "I'll call the hearing tech and schedule the hearing test."

An hour later, a woman knocks on the open door and rolls a metal cart into the room. On the cart is a computer monitor and hearing test equipment. The woman's brown hair hangs at her shoulders, and she wears a flowery hospital shirt and jeans and white shoes. She glues rubber cups over Avery's ears and punches data into the computer.

"What's his name?" she asks.

"Avery Graf Groneberg."

"How old is he?"

"Five weeks," I say. "Him and his twin brother were born seven weeks early."

"Does he have any problems that you know of?"

"He has Down syndrome," I say.

The woman pushes a few buttons on the machine. "My son weighed two pounds when he was born," she says, matter-of-factly. "We spent the first three months in the hospital." She goes on to tell me about her son. He is fifteen, but looks like he's ten. He still has babysitters. He wears a helmet. She says, "You get thick skin. I've found that it isn't good or bad, it's just different."

After the hearing test, Avery is finally ready to leave. It feels as if I am kidnapping my own son, as if he really belongs to the hospital, not to Jennifer and me. With Avery in the car seat and the monitor slung over my shoulder like a heavy black purse with a pulse, I take the elevator to the ground floor. At the snack shop, I buy one last pack of pink-and-white sparkle cookies for Carter, then walk through the revolving door, out into the day.

Just north of town, I merge onto Highway 93, headed for home. A hitchhiker with a guitar strapped around his neck and a duffle bag at his feet stands on the shoulder of the road. I speed past and he raises his arms as if to ask, "Why not, man? What's the hurry, where's the risk?" But

I can't stop, can't even slow down enough to point in the backseat or mouth the words "I'm sorry." He can't see Avery, strapped into the car seat in the back, the monitor blinking away on the passenger's seat. I drive.

Three motorcycles form a moving triangle in the north-bound lane ahead of me. One guy is way out front, the other two staggered behind. They roar north and I follow.

It's not a prayer that runs through my head, more of a blessing or a confession. I think of the words *retardation, hope, genetics, forgiveness*. They cancel one another out. The up, the down, the left and right. The good, the bad, the different. I ask that we all be forgiven, that we all be given a second chance in this life.

Ahead, the roar of motorcycles pulsing like the chanting of monks. The green light of the monitor, my son's heart, blinks *GO, GO, GO*. With our hearts wide open, we are going home.

I turn off the lights in the office, grab a halter and lead rope, and head outside into the gray light. The clouds hang low over Chief Cliff and the Salish Range. It is raining lightly, nearly cold enough to snow. There are still marks on the colt's nose and cheeks where the old halter rubbed his winter coat off, but they disappear when I halter him and tie him to a post. I run the comb over his back and neck and sides and try to tame his unruly mane and tail. I lift each of his front hooves in turn and scrape them clean, then run my hand along the colt's back and down his left hip, working my way down his leg. He dances away, so his right side is up against the wooden rails of the pen. "Quit!" I scold.

The afternoon wind is blowing off the lake and a cold rain mists down. Maybe it's the unsettled weather that is bothering the colt, but at this point, I don't really care. This isn't really a partnership and it's not all sunshine and sweet feed. If I want his hoof, I'll have it. He is up against the rails of the pen now, so I've got him trapped. "Hey, boy," I whisper, and run my hand down his left leg again. He switches me in the face with his ratty tail. He lifts his leg and stamps it down, then pushes me aside with his hindquarters. I try again and again, getting more frustrated with each failed attempt. And each time, the colt seems a little more apt to kick me. It's come to this. I go to the barn for the rope.

These days, it's called "gentling" or "starting" or "training" a horse. "Breaking" conjures up images of bloody ropes and whips and wild-eyed fear. But some part of me wants a fight. I want to go toe to toe with something, to grit my teeth and strike back, to make up for all of the times last summer when I had to take what was handed to me. But that isn't fair to the colt. None of it is fair.

I come back with a black-and-white nylon rope, stripped like a candy cane. I tie a loop in one end, pass it between the colt's hind legs, and run the other end of the rope through the loop. I drop it over his left rear hock, just above the hoof, take a wrap around a fence post behind him, and pull the slack out of the rope until the hoof is just a few inches off the ground, like I saw Forrest do with the stallion. The colt doesn't seem to mind. I tie it off and wait. He is more patient than I am. After five minutes, I untie the rope from the post and ease his foot to the ground.

Then I start at his head and work my way back, petting his flank, talking to him, working my way down. He lets me pick up his left rear hoof and rest it on my leg. One hand holding the rough wall of his hoof, I reach into my back pocket for the pick and I clean the sole, feeling his history etched there. When I am done, I try to pick up the colt's right rear, but he shifts all of his weight to that leg. I concede. I stroke the colt's neck and tell him he did good. It is enough for today.

Finally, Montana. He rides in the back of the wagon, sicker than sick from drinking bad water in Wyoming. His stomach knots and comes loose time and again, heaving up nothing. His clothes are ruined, caked and smelling of his sickness. It's October and he made it to the promised land.

When they get to Armell's Creek, just eight miles south of the Yellowstone, there is nothing but the narrow, muddy creek lined with cottonwoods, their leaves already turning. A crew goes to work building corrals, outbuildings, bunkhouses, and rough furniture. Teddy and the other cowboys sleep in tents at night, and spend their days trying to keep the cattle from straying. He wants to see the Yellowstone so badly after coming all this way, seventeen hundred miles from San Antonio to here. He considers making a run for it, eight miles north and back, just to see the river he has dreamed about all this time.

The boss pays off the crew, but doesn't give them the chance to spend their hard-earned wages. He invites a

Presbyterian preacher and his daughter from Miles City to come out and save anyone who needs saving. Instead of celebrating Montana, the men huddle around the fire, singing hymns they remember their mothers singing. The preacher's daughter's eyes glow like coals. The men's hearts beat faster with her beauty.

The boss sends Teddy south with a string of pack horses. He rides through the Crow territory where Custer met his fate seven years earlier, and hunts horses the outfit had lost along the way. Teddy makes a sweep down to the Wyoming line, gathering what he can, then he turns and heads back north, up the Tongue River toward Miles City. In the mornings, camped over his little fire, Teddy can feel winter in his bones. He's known February blizzards back in Lincoln, but he doesn't know what to expect from Montana. It's such a new land, so far north.

When he finally makes it to Miles City with the pack string and the half dozen runaway horses, Teddy pens them at Ringer & Johnson's livery on Main. He doesn't even stop for a drink of whiskey or a hot meal or the temptation of the sporting girls. Teddy rides Little Billy north, following the cottonwood trees that line the Tongue River. And finally, there it is, the Yellowstone. The water is the color of a tarnished knife blade, running fast and cold. There, at the bank of the mighty river, Teddy swings down from the saddle and leads his best horse into the current, just so he can feel the water against his skin, to know that it is real. They have made it.

It is one of those days when the babies aren't interested in taking a nap, and Carter is at loose ends. Jennifer and I load the kids into the car and drive. The boys are asleep by the time we hit the intersection with the highway across from the fire hall.

"Do you want to go see the horse?" I ask.

"Really?" Jennifer jokes. "You're going to introduce me to the other love in your life?"

"Very funny," I say, turning on the blinker signal and heading south, toward town. The drive there will eat up the better part of an hour, and the boys should sleep the entire way.

When I pull the car off the highway onto the rutted gravel of Bob's road, Carter rubs his eyes, looking around, Avery and Bennett stirring on each side of him.

"We're going to look at Daddy's horse," Jennifer explains.

At the barn, I set up the double stroller while Jennifer gets the boys out of their car seats. Then, while Jennifer buckles Avery and Bennett into the stroller, Carter and I go to the barn for a halter and rope.

"It's lucky you have a horse," Carter says.

I don't want to ruin the beauty of the statement by asking him what he means, so I say, "Yes, it is." We walk to the pen alongside the arena and Jennifer is there with the stroller, looking at the colt.

"He's kind of scrawny, don't you think?" she asks.

It hurts my feelings, that her first thought isn't about how beautiful the colt is. I feel alone, as if I've made a huge mistake in buying the colt, and a smaller one in trying to share him with my family. I don't say a thing, my silence telling Jennifer that I've taken offense at her comment. I slip through the rails of the pen, then halter the colt, and tie him up. He is still thin, but he's come a long way since I first brought him here.

Jennifer says, "I just meant he was a little thin, is all."

"Yep" is all I say. Jennifer pushes the stroller to check out the arena and the outhouse, Carter following along. The other horses filter down the hill through the trees, drawn by the sound of our car. I brush the colt, hoping to make him look better. I know I shouldn't be so defensive, especially with Jennifer, but these days I seem to be hypersensitive about people making judgments based on first looks. I need to get over it.

When I'm done brushing the colt, I turn to see Jennifer, Carter, and the stroller with the boys surrounded by a half-dozen Oberlanders, my family dwarfed by the huge, golden horses.

I slip back through the rails of the pen and walk over, careful not to spook the herd. "This one is Digger," I say, patting one of the Oberlander geldings on the neck. "And this other is his partner, Nuff." I try to remember all of the horses' names that Bob told me. There are Pete and Mary, the matched black team. The cream-colored pony, Coco, and the donkey, Eeyore. There is Jesus, the stocky Oberlander cross, born on Christmas Eve two years ago. I pick Carter up and set him on the donkey's back, holding him in case the little burro bolts. But Eeyore just lays his ears back and stands there, waiting patiently.

"Wee-haw," Carter says, smiling, holding one hand in the air.

"There's some goats running around the place, too," I say. "They're probably camped out on the haystack." When I pick Carter up and set him on the ground, the donkey moves off, bossing some of the larger horses, nipping at their hind feet.

"What's your horse's name?" Carter asks.

"I don't know," I admit. "What do you think we should call him?"

Carter thinks for a second, squinting over at the colt. "Brownie."

"That's a good name for him," I say. "Maybe we can bake him some brownies and feed them to him next time we come out. You think he'd like that?"

The horses are moving off now, back up the hill to the pond, disappearing as quickly and as quietly as they came.

As we are driving out, a killdeer runs down the gravel road ahead of the car. The small brown-and-white bird with the black band around its neck runs along, dragging its wing, trying to protect a nest somewhere by laying down its life, saying "Take me," long after the danger has passed.

★　★　★

Dr. Burnett is a big man, weighing two hundred and seventy-five pounds and standing well over six feet tall. He is a retired osteopath from Alpine, New Jersey. His wife, Cora, is heiress to the Timken Roller Bearing fortune. The couple lives in a compound in the woods above the Hudson River, near the Palisades of New Jersey. Here Burnett pursues his medical research. He dreams of using electromagnetism to cure cancer, to prolong human life. His laboratory is constructed of entirely nonmagnetic materials so the building won't interfere with his experiments. The roof is made of copper. Then, on March 12, 1939, while the couple is away visiting another cancer researcher, the laboratory burns to the ground in a mysterious fire.

Four years later, Dr. Burnett discovers Wild Horse Island. The isolation, the quiet, is perfect. But the Burnetts don't want to buy any property on the island unless they can own the thing in its entirety. The state of Montana still owns a thirty-six-acre tract of land it won't relinquish. Eventually, the Burnetts relent and, on September 8, 1943, they write Lewis Penwell a check. The Burnetts get all of the land, the wildlife, Hiawatha Lodge, the home Penwell built for his son, guest cabins, the boats, everything. Dr. Burnett has his own ideas about horses and he doesn't want the eight that roam the island. The palomino stallion, the scrubby homesteader mares, Edgington's saddle horses, they all must go unwanted.

Penwell hires men to trap the horses in a corral. A small flat-decked barge, pulled by another boat, is lined up to transport them to the mainland. Though the barge is only large enough to handle three horses safely, all eight are led onto the deck and tied to a ring in the center of the deck. The barge chugs toward the mainland a mile in the distance. The lake rises and falls, water breaking over the surface of the barge. A wave tips the barge into the air, knocking the horses to the other side. This shifting weight flips the barge upside down, and all of the horses hang, like eight four-legged anchors, under the water. Fred Penwell, Lewis's son, dives into the water with his knife. He swims under the barge and cuts the horses free, dodging the slow-moving frantic legs and hooves. The horses break the surface, swim to the island, and run for the hills.

Dr. Burnett loves the island and spends as much time as he can there. His wife, Cora, is older, a sculptor and collector of rare art. She could care less about the island in Montana. She spends one summer there and never returns. Burnett loves to ride Chief, his half-Thoroughbred, half-Percheron sorrel around the property. He buys a purebred Arabian stallion and some good brood mares with the objective of raising quality saddle horses. Then he pays more than thirty thousand dollars for Riskulus, a chestnut stallion out of the famed sire Stimulus, from Calumet Farm in Lexington, Kentucky. Riskulus was scratched just before the running of the sixtieth Kentucky Derby in 1934. As a four-year-old, Riskulus sets the mile and an eighth track record at Santa Anita. And ten years later he is penned up on Wild Horse Island in northwest Montana, used only to breed a select few mares.

On June 3, 1946, Burnett finally secures the thirty-six acres owned by the state of Montana. Now he owns all of Wild Horse Island. He revels in it. He tells some local friends, "You fellows don't know what you have here. Montana sunshine is the finest in the world and I've been all over most of it."

The animals on the island are thriving. By the fall of 1954, there are about one hundred bighorn sheep on the island, and between three to four hundred head of deer. Burnett's horse herd numbers more than a hundred head. The native grasses have been decimated. Burnett decides to cull the horse herd by half. And, in December 1954, sixty men volunteer to help Montana Fish and Game trap and transplant a dozen bighorn sheep. They gather a dozen, mostly young animals, which are moved one hundred miles northwest, to an area outside of Libby, Montana.

The next summer, 1955, burns hot. The island's remaining horses overgraze the sparse grass. Then it starts to snow in late October. The temperatures plummet, the wind howls like a hungry thing. A crust forms over the snow and the horses cannot paw through it to what little grass is below. That January, Cora Timken Burnett dies in New Jersey and leaves her husband with a hole in his heart and a huge fortune, estimated at somewhere in the neighborhood of $55 million ($360 million today). Dr. Burnett never visits Wild Horse Island again.

A month later, the island is covered in twenty-six inches of crusted snow. The horses chew on dead sagebrush. Burnett finally hires an airplane to drop hay to the starving horses. By the end of the winter, only a pair of horses and a mule have survived.

A mare in heat stands under the moonlight on the little hill just across from the barn. The overhead door has been accidentally left open. The stallion squeals, then spins and kicks the stall door with both hind feet.

In the pen by the arena, the colt lifts his head at the sound of hooves against wood, and turns toward the barn. Out on the highway, a truck downshifts, coming down the long incline into Elmo. The stallion squeals again, and spins and kicks the door, the sound echoing in the barn and reaching the colt. He can smell the mare in heat, can see her silhouette on the hill by the barn, surrounded by other horses.

The stallion squeals and kicks once more. This time the stall door explodes open. The sound of hooves on concrete, wire screeching, and the horses thunder up the hill, away from the brown colt.

Soon there is the tiny buzz of an engine starting up. It gets louder, coming down the hill toward the barn, and the colt sees two pinpricks of light in the blackness, getting larger. The man pulls the machine up to the barn door. He turns on the overhead lights, discovers the broken stall door, and he asks, "What the bejesus?"

★　　★　　★

"I had a hell of a night," Bob says. He looks spent, the color in his eyes faded. "The stud busted out of his stall and went on a tear. He got all cut up."

We walk to the stall. "Look at this," Bob says, pointing at the bent bolt on the latch of the stall door. "I hammered it straight as best I could, but I'm going to have to replace it."

"He kicked the door open?" I ask. I can't imagine the horse would know just where to kick.

"Yeah," Bob answers. "I forgot to close the overhead door last night and one of the mares must have been in heat. She needed breeding anyway, but look at Schloss." He turns on the light and the stallion stands there, dried white sweat on his hide, greasy yellow salve on a shallow gash across his chest, more on his hindquarters. "He must have been running through wire all night. I finally opened the big gate on the round corral and herded him in there and caught him. I called the vet and he told me to put some goop on the cuts. I just finished when you pulled up."

Earlier Bob told me he'd teach me what he knew about join-up and natural horsemanship. These days, trust and patience and communication have replaced the ropes and slickers and war bridles of the past.

"We don't have to work on join-up today," I say. "Let's do it some other time."

"No, let's do it now," Bob says. "Once you join-up with him, everything else will go better. I want you to learn this."

The round corral is made of twenty-eight posts, set ten feet apart, with three rails running horizontally across. "It's seventy feet wide," Bob says. "A little big for what we're trying to do, but it'll still work." Bob stands inside the corral with my colt, and I'm outside, looking through the rails. Bob unsnaps the lead from the colt's black halter, then steps back and begins swinging the rope in big overhand circles, moving toward the horse's rear. The colt starts trotting clockwise around the perimeter of the corral.

"You want to be in the right place, just back enough so that you don't stop him," Bob says. "And keep moving as he moves, so that you're always in the right spot." The colt keeps trotting, head up, tail out. After seven rounds, Bob stops swinging the rope and steps ahead. The colt stops. Bob extends his free hand, turns sideways, and hangs his head. He looks at the colt from the corner of his eye, from under his cowboy hat. The colt looks away. Bob straightens and starts swinging the rope again, moving the colt in the same direction. "Start him moving again as soon as he breaks eye contact."

The colt trots around and around. The rope swings in circles. Clouds slide across the sky above. I'm not sure what any of this is supposed to accomplish. It seems to me that Bob is teaching the colt how to move away from swinging ropes.

Bob drops the rope and slouches up to the colt once again. The horse stares and lets Bob get within a foot of him before walking off.

"He may not take very long," Bob says. "If we had a smaller corral, it'd go a lot quicker." He opens the gate to the corral and steps through, holding the rope out to me. "It's your turn," he says.

"What happens once I get up to him?" I ask, taking the rope.

"Pet him and praise him, then take a few steps away and he ought to follow. Just go slow. I'm going to go check on Schloss."

The colt and I watch Bob walk back to the barn.

I close the gate behind me and latch it, then turn and cluck my tongue and begin swinging the rope. The colt trots around the corral. I count five circuits, then let the rope fall and hold it behind my back. I approach the horse, my free hand stretched toward him. He is breathing hard. I drop my head a little, inch up to the horse sideways, trying to mimic Bob's movements. The colt's looking at me, watching my hand as it reaches up. I stroke his neck, praise him in whispers, saying, "Good boy." I've touched him all those times before while brushing him, but this is different. He is not tied to anything. His eyes look so deep and dark and brown. When I turn and walk off two steps, he does not follow. Bob said he should follow.

I turn back to the colt. He is waiting. I swing the rope again to get him moving. And now, each time I try to stop him and get him to lock on, he looks away toward the barn and walks off.

Bob returns and sits on the ground with his legs stretched out in front of him, watching.

"I was really close," I say. "I had him and I lost him."

"Try going the other direction once in a while," he says. "And just be sure to end the day five minutes before you want to. Always quit on a positive note."

I make the colt go counterclockwise this time. One, two, three, four, five trips around. Then I drop the rope and he stops and I walk up to him slowly, reaching out to him. He lets me stroke his neck and I say, "Good boy," but he still doesn't follow when I walk off.

"He was ready to stop back there, but you sort of missed the cue and kept him running," Bob says. "But that's all right. You got a really mellow horse. I like his disposition."

I climb through the corral rails and sit down next to Bob. My arm is sore from swinging the rope so much. We watch the colt as he sniffs the ground, folds his legs under him, drops to the sand, and rolls.

"Once I asked Forrest what he thought of all this join-up and horse-whisperer stuff and he said he thought it was good. I figured he'd tell me it was all a bunch of hogwash, but he said, in the old days, they never had much time to spend training a horse, so they had to do whatever it took."

The colt rolls again and his feet get caught between the middle and bottom rails of the corral. As he tries to stand, he knocks off the middle rail with his neck and back. It happens so fast that Bob and I can do nothing but watch. And now the colt is outside the corral, running free with the other horses, the Oberlanders and the saddle horses and the donkey.

We walk to the barn and get the Gator. Bob drives and I'm in the passenger's seat, holding a lead rope and a coffee can full of sweet feed. While the colt was penned up, the other horses were able to smell him and get used to a new animal in their midst, but now that he is loose, the herd strings out behind the colt, chasing him around the lower pasture. Jesus is the worst, racing in to bite the colt on his haunches. We finally manage to separate the colt from the other horses in the corner of the pasture. His hindquarters are frothy with sweat. He is breathing hard. He looks across the barbed wire, considering the merits of jumping the fence. And then, as I am walking toward him shaking the can of sweet feed to bribe him, the colt spins and runs past us. We are back in the Gator, bombing around the field, dodging rocks and the occasional pine tree. Bob leans over and says, "He's got a nice gait."

Teddy is wild from so much time in the country. It's been six months since he left Texas. No, seven. He's got seven hundred dollars, some of it wages, the rest the remains of his inheritance. Saloons and music halls line Miles City's main street, the girls coming and going like lights blinking on and off and on. At Turner's Tivoli Theater, a redhead keeps trying to get him to buy a five-dollar bottle of wine, overpriced and watered down, but he can't stop looking at her, her red hair like flames dancing. Her tights and short skirt. She looks like something from a sleep-deprived daydream, not real at all. She whispers, "There's a crib in back if that's more to your liking." Teddy nods and follows her down the stairs to a dark hallway behind the stage. The band plays "Clementine." *You are lost and gone forever, dreadful sorry, Clementine.* Teddy thinks of his money, thinks that this must be a con to rob him. With each step he senses danger, imagines a club bearing down on the back of his head. He spins on his heels and the spur on his left boot catches in the carpeting. He goes tumbling, arms outstretched, breaking though the paper screen onto the stage. The audience stares, wondering if this is part of the act.

Behind him, Teddy can hear the redhead gasp. He grabs a chair from the startled fiddle player, straddles it, and rides the chair across the stage, bucking and reeling and yelling, "Whoa, Blue! Whoa, Blue!"

The audience roars. Someone in the crowd throws an empty bottle and it clatters across the stage, disappearing behind the torn screen. A pistol is fired into the air. The manager yells, "Hey, Blue, you come out of there."

And ever after he was Blue.

Teddy Blue.

The colt moves to the far corner of the pen at the boy's approach. He watches as the boy lifts the chain from its nail, opens the gate, walks into the pen, and pushes the gate closed behind. The boy puts the hose into the rubber feed dish, then lifts the handle on the hydrant. When the tub is filled with fresh water, he shuts off the hydrant and squeezes through the rails, back to the barn where his father is cleaning stalls.

Later that night, after everything has gone quiet except for the sound of crickets and the shimmer of satellites and stars filling the black sky, the colt backs up to the gate and rubs his haunches on the rough wood. Something gives and he backs up another step, wanting to scratch his itch. He feels nothing but space. The colt turns to find the gate swinging open on its hinges. He steps into the night.

Bob phones and says, "I went down with the kids last night before taking them back to their mother's place. Robbie couldn't believe that he's the same horse you brought here. And Molly wanted to know what his name is. We'll have to get him a name."

"You're right," I say. "Carter said I should call him 'Brownie,' but I just keep calling him 'Boy' or 'Bud.' I'll have to think of something better than that."

"Well, the reason I called, I'm afraid something got left open last night and your colt took off. He is running with the herd again."

"Oh, okay," I say. "I'll head over now and try to catch him."

"Use the Gator," Bob says. "He should know the routine by now."

I drive through Bob's place to the barn. The colt's pen is empty. I look around the side of the barn and see the goats camped out on the haystack. Leroy and his mother and the stallion are in their respective stalls, but the other horses are nowhere in sight.

I clean the stalls in the barn and dump the manure in the spreader. Then I freshen each stall with a wheelbarrowload of sawdust from the pile near the haystack. I don't even really care if I catch the colt. I'm not sure why I bought him in the first place. I drive all this way, every day, just to feed and water him. We've only taken the tiniest steps forward together. I steer the wheelbarrow out to the colt's pen and fork up the piles of manure there. Then I wheel it over to the round corral. I open the big gate and sift a few horse crapples from the sand.

Something moves directly behind me. I duck, involuntarily, imagining that Bob has snuck up behind me or a hawk is descending to strike at my head. I turn and he is there. The colt. None of the other horses are in sight. He is looking only for me. I drop the wood-handled manure fork and reach up and stroke his neck. I scratch the place he likes, right at the base of his withers. He drops his head and turns to one side a little, like a dog about to start thumping the ground with his foot. "Hey, Boy," I say.

I think about how, more often than not, when we are trying to be generous with others, we end up giving them the wrong things. We give them what we want for our own. But here, the colt has given me exactly what I needed. He has given me himself.

Bob said that I need to get this colt a name, but I already know what it is. He isn't the black colt any longer. And he isn't Brownie or Bud or Boy. He is Blue.

Chapter Four

THERE IS A WAY TO TRAIN A HORSE WHERE
WHEN YOU GET DONE, YOU'VE GOT THE HORSE
ON HIS OWN GROUND. A GOOD HORSE WILL
FIGURE THINGS OUT ON HIS OWN. YOU CAN
SEE WHAT'S IN HIS HEART. HE WON'T DO ONE
THING WHILE YOU'RE WATCHING HIM AND
ANOTHER WHEN YOU AIN'T. HE'S ALL OF A
PIECE. WHEN YOU GET A HORSE TO THAT
PLACE YOU CAN'T HARDLY GET HIM TO DO
SOMETHING HE KNOWS IS WRONG. HE'LL
FIGHT YOU OVER IT. AND IF YOU MISTREAT
HIM, IT JUST ABOUT KILLS HIM. A GOOD HORSE
HAS JUSTICE IN HIS HEART. I'VE SEEN IT.

—CORMAC MCCARTHY,
Cities of the Plain

The morning light reaches the colt sooner than it had
when he lived closer to the mountains. The first seam of
silver over the Missions warming the bare rock of Chief
Cliff, the night's shadows lifting and lengthening, the
dew drying on the blades of grass. A flock of blackbirds,

dozens of them, wings overhead in the dawn sky, heading south. The breeze pushes off of the lake, carrying the smells of town. Cooked bacon and stray dogs and laundry hung out to dry.

On the hill above the barn, there is the sound of the tiny engine, the man driving the cart down from the house. He sings while he feeds the horses in the barn, the tenor voice booming from the overhead door like an auditorium. "Il sole allegramente batte ai tuoi vetri." *The sun joyfully taps at your windows.* "Amor pian pian batte al tuo cuore." *Love very softly taps at your heart.* "E l'uno e l'altro chiama." *And they are both calling you.*

The man feeds the colt last, walking over to the pen and pouring a half can of grain into the rubber feed dish, then tossing some hay onto the ground. *"Buon giorno, puledro,"* he says. "You're finally starting to look like a horse, aren't you?" He fills the colt's water dish, then walks over to the barn, gets in the cart, and disappears up the hill.

The colt hears a trio of dogs barking to the north, near the small town. A school bus stops on the highway, lights flashing. It is a new day.

Later, the other horses graze past the pen. The golden mares and their flaxen foals come to lick the salt block near the barn. The donkey follows, trailing one of the big geldings. Later still, the saddle horses arrive. Once in a while, the colt catches a glimpse of the goats as they sneak through the fence to lie on the stack of hay bales in the lean-to against the big red barn during the heat of the day, their goat stench drifting over to him. Flies buzz. The grass grows wild. The colt is at home in this world.

One Good Horse

When I drive down the road past Bob's house and through the timbered hillside to the barn, I see that a small circle of portable metal panels has been set up inside the big round corral. Bob had mentioned that he wanted to get a smaller corral for working his own horses. The metallic brown paint gleams in the sun. Seeing the new training pen prods me. I realize this is real, this is what I should be working toward.

I halter Blue and start brushing him. It is a ritual. He is coming into himself. The last of his winter coat is gone, and his sleek dark brown hair shimmers, lighter around the muzzle. He is filling out and, finally, I can't see his ribs anymore. It's good that I'm taking my time with him. There is no rush, and this is the only time I'll ever do this. I won't become a horse trainer, won't do any of it again.

I walk from his pen to my truck and return with a saddle pad and my chinks, short leather-fringed chaps. I let the colt sniff the pad. I know it smells of Draco and Dipper, the horses on Phil's ranch where I used to work. I've kept the pad in the backseat of my truck for the last year. It's a cowboy's air freshener, a reminder of the work that I love and long for.

Blue nibbles the corner of the pad, mouthing it gently. I rub the pad along his neck, his back, his haunches, ready for his reaction. Nothing. I lay it on his back, but he doesn't care. I take off the pad and pick up the chinks, figuring the leather fringe and the jingle of the six chrome buckles might scare him. I hold the chinks out to the colt.

He smells them, pulls at a string of fringe with his teeth. I rub him down with the chinks, moving them up to his neck, back to his hips, down to his rear. Nothing. Again I put the saddle pad on his back then hang the chinks over the pad, like two empty legs straddling him. He flicks his ears at a horsefly.

"Blue," I say. He looks up at the sound of my voice, but I can't think of anything else to say. I pat him on the neck, take the chinks and saddle pad off his back, and hang them on the rail behind him.

I unlatch the gate and walk over to look at the new round pen. It consists of eight brown metal panels, each twelve feet long and six feet high. A four-foot-wide gate opens to the interior. It looks like a round boxing ring, a fitting place for a fight. This is where I will ride Blue for the first time.

It's been seven years since I rode a saddle bronc in the Bucking Horse Sale back in Miles City. I knew nothing about the history of the horse I was getting on, only what the announcer said as I settled down onto the horse's back. She was a mare from Canada. I only stayed with the bronc for a few jumps out of the chute before I was thrown to the dirt of the arena. There were a thousand people watching. Tourists, neighbors, rodeo cowboys who actually knew how to ride broncs, and the rodeo stock contractors who were bidding on the horses.

It was such a public display. I know now that I was trying to prove myself, to prove that I fit with the locals who had been riding horses all their lives. I have the nagging feeling that I am doing the same thing with Blue now. I'm longing for a battle of wills, wishing that he'll try to buck me off and hoping that I'm up to the test. Even though it will be a private rodeo, I am looking forward to it. And though I'm spoiling for a fight, I'm afraid there will be no battles here, no do-overs. Blue has shown me nothing but a sort of bored tolerance.

Behind me, I hear the colt snort. I turn and see him leaning back on the lead rope, straining to get a look at what is behind him. The breeze plays with the fringe on the legs of the chinks. It's the first time I've seen Blue alarmed. He moves from side to side, more curious now than afraid. I watch him for a while to make sure he isn't going to come unglued, then I walk to the truck to get my saddle.

Teddy has never been this scared in his life. It's not just the Indians, it's that he's cold and—though there is a full moon—dawn is still hours away. He huddles on the cut bank above the icy flow of the Rosebud at the mouth of Lame Deer Creek, pointing his six-shooter toward the half dozen teepees just seventy-five yards off. Another FUF cowboy creeps up next to him and tries to hide behind a bit of sagebrush sticking up from the frozen soil. Teddy can see fear lighting his partner's eyes. Teddy promises himself, if he gets out of this alive, he will quit the FUF and join an honest-to-goodness outfit, one that won't send him out to shoot innocent Indians.

They're in this jackpot over a stunt one of Zook and Alderson's hired hands pulled. The fellow was some mudsill from Kentucky named Sawney Tolliver. The Cheyenne were camping in the area, and one of them, a tall warrior named Black Wolf, had eaten dinner at the Zook Ranch, then lay down to digest his meal, placing his black stovepipe hat across his eyes. Tolliver stood in the doorway of the bunkhouse, loading his gun. He turned to another cowboy behind him and said, "Dollar says I kin knock that hat offa that old boy's head." Not having the dollar in question, Tolliver coppered his bet by aiming a little low. The stovepipe hat toppled off the Indian, then he let out a ghastly groan and rolled over. Tolliver didn't even think to collect his winnings. He mounted up alongside the other cowboy and they rode to a neighboring ranch for help, knowing when word got out that they had murdered a Cheyenne, all hell would come raining down.

Black Wolf was merely knocked unconscious from the bullet that parted his coal black hair. When he came to, the warrior rode back to the mouth of Lame Deer Creek, to the seven lodges there, and he told the others what had happened. Some of the women attended to his wound, tying an enormous hat of dried buffalo dung to his bloody head. A dozen other warriors rode to the ranch, shot Zook's best cow dog, set fire to the ranch house, and, figuring they were even, returned to their camp.

A dollar bet and a piss-poor shot. Cold and tired from riding all night, Teddy knows it can only end badly. When the sky just lightens at the horizon, Teddy and the others hear the voice of an old warrior praying to the sun for justice that may or may not come. He is silhouetted now, on the tall hill above the creek, and the old man's voice makes Teddy want to weep with shame.

At dawn, the deputy and Frank Thompson, an old scout from Fort Keogh, ride into the camp and talk things over with Black Wolf, who is still wearing the big buffalo chip on his head. Blood has dried on the side of the man's neck. Although there are more than three hundred Cheyenne camped six miles up the Rosebud, and even though they feel they have done nothing wrong, Black Wolf agrees to be taken to Miles City, along with twelve other men, to stand trial. By now, Sawney Tolliver is already across the Wyoming line, riding hard, and not looking back.

Teddy and five other men escort the Indians up the Rosebud to the rail line in Forsyth. One of the warriors, the big one they call Pine, sits next to Teddy in the open-slatted cattle car on the train. Before they reach Miles City, Pine takes something from his pocket and hands it to Teddy, who has given him food and drink the entire way. It is a small silver ring, inscribed with C CO 7 CAV. The C Company of the Seventh Cavalry, under Custer, rode sorrel horses. The ring is too small for even Teddy's smallest finger, so he puts it in his pocket. Every time he sees the small circle of silver, he remembers the old Indian on the hill, praying to the new day sun.

I walk back to the pen carrying the saddle against my hip. Blue looks at me wide-eyed, still a little alarmed from the breeze playing with the fringe on my chinks. "It's okay," I say. "Easy now." I throw the saddle over the top rail of the pen, unbuckle the rear cinch and hang it on the rail, then tie the long saddle strings on each side in a loose knot, so they don't startle Blue.

I approach the colt, rubbing him down with the chinks again until he doesn't care about them anymore. Then I take the pad and lay it across his back. Finally, I bring the saddle down from the top rail and heave it up onto Blue's back. He doesn't even blink. I walk around to the off side and lower the cinch and stirrup. Back on the other side, I reach under his belly for the end of the cinch. I've done this enough times with other horses that I don't have to look at my hands. Instead, I watch Blue. I want to go slow, want to give him time to get used to the saddle, though he shows no concern, nothing but a sort of sleepiness.

I could go back to the barn and clean stalls, but I want to be able to watch Blue, in case he gets scared again. I walk around to the tiny copper-roofed building on the other side of the arena. The narrow two-story building is painted red and there is a door on each level. The word FREE is painted on the ground-level door. I push it open and see a small chemical toilet inside. Up the flight of stairs, the second-story door has TWENTY-FIVE CENTS painted on it. I stand on the little balcony of the two-story outhouse, looking out over the arena. The colt, tied to the post, looks half asleep. Beyond, I see Chief Cliff.

Legend has it that Big Knife, Chief of the Kootenais, had become disheartened that the young braves of his tribe no longer consulted with the elders, no longer followed the ways of the past. One summer evening, the chief dressed in his best clothes, the headdress and the buckskin outfit. He adorned his pony with feathers and paint, then rode up to the edge of the cliff. Big Knife called out, *Hear me, my people. My heart is heavy with grief. You have forgotten the teachings of your elders. You have forgotten their brave deeds and generous acts. Only ill luck and misery will come to those who forsake the laws and teachings of the elders of the tribe. Knowing that, I make this one last effort to remind you of the bravery and wisdom of your grandfathers.* Below, his tribe danced and played games, unconcerned with the actions of the old chief. He turned his horse and began to guide it slowly down, back to his people and their songs and games. Then the chief stopped. Words were not enough. The old man spun his horse around and galloped back up the hill. At a dead run, the chief raced his horse over the edge of the cliff. The people stopped and looked up. Fringe and feathers and mane and tail hanging in the air, then hooves clattering against rock, hide scraping, bones breaking.

Now, just south of Chief Cliff, freshly graveled roads vein the grassy field. Near the new split rail fence along the highway, a sign reads: CHIEF CLIFF ESTATES. PUT A LITTLE PIECE OF MONTANA IN YOUR RETIREMENT ACCOUNT. I think of the old chief telling his people to honor the ways of the past. I think of retirement accounts and sacred ground, of careless dancing and broken horses. None of us are innocent. I have no answers. I walk down from the balcony of the copper-roofed outhouse, back to my colt.

His eyelids are heavy and his head droops. He dozes, unconcerned. I click my tongue, so as not to scare him. "Hey, Blue," I say, and he opens his eyes and turns his head toward me. I walk the colt around the pen, letting him get used to the weight of the saddle. Around and around. I lead him close to the rails of the pen, knocking stirrups into fence posts, testing his tolerance. No problem. I untie the long saddle strings and let them fall against his flanks, but he isn't bothered by them. I get the rear cinch from the rail it hangs on and buckle it back to the off-side billet, then run it under the horse's belly and buckle it loosely. He is okay with all of it. I can't help but think he's either a little slow, or he's still wormy, or he's already broke.

While they are gathering the other loose horses one morning, Teddy's horse spooks. It rears up and pitches him down onto a cottonwood log. Teddy can feel his back knot with extraordinary pain, but he mounts the horse and goes back to work. They are on the Mizpah gather, each outfit sorting their cattle from the bunch, branding the slick calves, taking a tally. The next morning, Teddy's back is so bad, he can't even stand. The N Bar boys lift him into a wagon and haul him north, to Miles City, to recuperate in a room there.

As he lies in bed, Teddy remembers the time, almost a year ago, when that boy from the FUF died. He was a lunger, a victim of tuberculosis. He wasn't a cowboy at all, just an accountant from the ranch office in St. Paul, out to recuperate in the fresh western air. When the TB came back, the boss sent him to Miles City with Teddy as an escort. The blood he coughed up day and night. The *Miles City Star* laid out on the floor didn't help keep anything clean. The boy would only sleep when he could lay his head on Teddy's arm. Teddy thought of his own brother, Jimmy, dying so many years ago back in Lincoln. His hat blowing in the grave. Finally, a week later, it was over. They boxed the accountant up and put him on the train, back to his family in Boston.

Teddy quit the FUF in the spring, and it was a long time coming. They wouldn't feed their cowboys anything but beans and cornmeal and some condemned pork salvaged from Fort Keogh, something not even fit for soldiers to eat. The FUF cowboys finally resorted to killing a steer and hiding it in the haystack, going out after dark to cut a few steaks off the carcass. When the boss found out, he fired the whole crew, then hired them back again that winter. Then there was that mess with Black Wolf and the Cheyenne.

Through May, June, and July, he worked for Matt Winter, an acquaintance from Nebraska, on the ranch Winter managed on Otter Creek, south of Miles City. But the horses were so damned rank. Every time he mounted any horse but his own Little Billy, Teddy had to reach up and bend the horse's ear over to distract the animal. Once he was up in the saddle, Teddy turned the horse's ear loose and hung on for his ever-blessed life.

Now he works for a real cow outfit, the Newman Brothers' N Bar Ranch. Zeke and Henry Newman were originally from St. Louis, but came west to make their fortune by securing government contracts to supply beef to Indian reservations. The Newmans were forced to move their cattle north and west because of settlers and range fires. They now have two ranges, one in the Powder River country, just north of the Wyoming border, and the other north, in the Big Dry county.

Teddy is more than just a common cowboy now. He is a rep, going from roundup to roundup, representing the N Bar at each gather. Teddy's got a good string of horses, the buckskin and the tall sorrel, the gray and the other gray, and Little Billy. He's got independence from his bosses, a reputation as a hard worker, a man who is fair and loyal to the outfit. He gets to visit with the other reps and their cowboys as he travels from grazing district to grazing district, telling stories and trading lies. And he is good at the work. The brands seared into his brains, he doesn't even know how many there are. Left rib, right hip, notched ears or not. He's been training for this job his entire life, like school lessons, since Lincoln. He knows them all, knows which cows belong to what outfit.

But even with the good horses, Teddy still got hurt, that horse rearing up and tossing him. He can't stand being in the small room, being indoors and remembering that dead FUF boy they boxed up in the bloody hotel room. He rises from the bed and hobbles down the stairs, out into the night air of Miles City. One shot of whiskey will loosen the knot in his back, will kill the pain between his ears and at the base of his neck.

A week later, when Zeke Newman is in town getting the payroll, he finds Teddy red-eyed and broke, cleaned of money and sobriety. He tells Teddy, "Time to head back to the gather, Blue."

Memorial Day. Bob is trimming an Oberlander mare in the shoeing stanchion when I pull up. Blue is tied in the big round corral alongside Jesus, the two-year-old Oberlander cross.

"Howdy, Mr. Tom," Bob says, wiping sweat from his brow.

"What do you know, Bob?"

"Not a heck of a lot." He looks up the hill. "Uh-oh, emergency."

I turn and see the Gator driven by a young girl.

"It can't be too bad," Bob says. "Robbie's got a Pop-Tart in his mouth."

Bob has his three kids, Robbie, Molly, and Ian, for the long weekend. They are twelve, eleven, and nine years old.

"What's up?" Bob asks when the kids pile out of the Gator.

"We just wanted to play down here," Molly says. They run into the barn and climb a rope ladder to the games above the office.

"I was thinking about working some of my green horses. You got time to throw a saddle on?" Bob asks me.

"Sure," I say.

I halter Blue and tie him alongside Jesus in the big round corral. "I think it's good for the other horses to watch what's going on and learn," Bob says. He is in the small round pen with Frisky, an Oberlander mare, who is saddled and ready to go. Bob talks to her softly. He holds the reins short, ready to pull her in a circle if she comes unhinged. He puts the toe of his cowboy boot into the left stirrup and hangs there, letting the horse feel his weight. Then he hoists himself up a little more, so he is lying across the saddle. The horse doesn't move. Bob swings his leg up and over the saddle and, in a matter of minutes, he is riding her in circles around the pen. Jesus, the big Oberlander cross, goes the same way. "Let's see if your horse is feeling any differently," Bob says.

I lead Blue into the little round pen. Bob hands me the bridle he used on the other horses, and holds on to the lead rope. The bridle is too big for my little horse. It slips over his ears easily. I slide my finger behind Blue's teeth and, when he starts gumming it, I slip the bit into his mouth and adjust the bridle so it fits correctly. The colt works his tongue over the bit, trying to spit it out. He cranes his neck and shakes his head. Bob takes the reins and unsnaps the rope from the halter. He tightens the cinch and asks, "Okay if I try him?"

"Go ahead," I say, with a twinge of uncertainty.

Bob goes through the same routine, putting a little weight in the stirrup, then leaning across the saddle. He pats the horse on the neck and, as he is about to swing his leg up, Bob slides down off the saddle and hands me the reins. "Let's just try that for a bit and see how he does," Bob says.

I go slow, talking to the colt the entire time, watching his ears, praying that he doesn't decide to smoke me. I step into the stirrup and his ears lie back a little, but he doesn't move. The colt is bunched up and I can feel him quivering. And then I am lying across the saddle like a dead man in an old Western.

"I think he'll do good for ya," Bob says. "Just make sure that I'm around when he's ready to be ridden. That way I can drive you to the hospital."

Later Bob cleans the stallion's stall while I pick through the sawdust in Leroy's. The little colt nibbles on my shirt while I sift through the sawdust in his stall. "How's Leroy doing?" I ask.

"The vet or the colt?" Bob asks.

"The colt."

"He seems to be coming along. I think we'll turn him out in the arena in a few days so he can get more exercise." I hear a muffled noise from the other stall and Bob scolds, "Ho, now Schloss."

"I want you to put together a list of chores for me," I say, "so that I can get some work done to repay you."

"I found some hay out your way," Bob says. "I'll give you a call one of these days and we can move a few tons. I'll put up the message board I bought, in the office, and jot down a few things for you to tackle."

"What do you hear from Forrest?" I ask.

"He's in the hospital," Bob says. "His son-in-law called me. Said it was dehydration, but they're watching him. One of these days I'm going to lock Forrest in a room with a tape recorder and not let him out until he's done telling me everything. I mean, once he's dead, that's it."

Memorial Day. I think of all the battles that we prepare for that are never fought, all of the fights that we never see coming. I think of Forrest Davis, twenty-one years old, holding his rifle on a landing craft, trying to see over the tall soldier in front of him. The Germans still used horses on the beaches of Normandy to haul their artillery from place to place. I hope the old man is all right.

★ ★ ★

We are early, and Avery has fallen asleep. I pull into the hospital lot and park. I unbuckle Avery and talk to him softly, waking him up. "C'mon, Bud," I say. "Time to go to work." When his eyes open, they are beautiful. Flecks of white, called Brushfield's spots, rim the dark blue irises like tiny waves in deep water. I pick Avery up and carry him to the side door of the hospital, the one marked PHYSICAL THERAPY.

The woman behind the reception desk looks up, smiles, and says, "Avery's here." She looks at the clock on the wall. "Take a seat. Wendy's just finishing with another patient. She'll be with you in a few minutes."

I sit in the little waiting room, holding Avery in my lap. There is a box of toys in the corner, a table loaded down with copies of *Reader's Digest* and old *TV Guide*s. Across the hall there is an open room with exercise equipment in it. On a counter along the wall, a portable stereo next to a plaster model of a human backbone.

I hold Avery low around the waist, like Jennifer showed me, so that he has to use his trunk muscles to support himself. I want to make a good impression on Wendy, the physical therapist, when she comes to get us.

Jennifer has been bringing Avery to his therapy appointments every Tuesday, but I asked her if it'd be all right if I brought him today. I want to know what happens at these sessions, want to know why Avery comes home so tired and what, if anything, I can do to help him. While Bennett is lurching around the house, Avery isn't even crawling yet. It hurts to see the difference between the two boys, to find myself comparing them.

Wendy has strawberry blond hair and a quick smile. She wears a pink top, white shorts, and tennis shoes. She could be the younger sister of the pediatrician who helped the boys out, a year ago, when they were born. It's unsettling being back in another hospital. We head down the hallway to the last room on the left. Inside, the air conditioner is going full blast. On the cream-colored walls, about three feet up, is a wallpaper banner with exotic animals printed on it. A zebra, tiger, giraffe, lion, repeating all the way around the room.

Wendy hands Avery a tiny wooden hammer, saying, "Here's his favorite toy." He grabs the hammer and bangs it on my kneecap. I bend around and look at his face and Avery is wearing his shy, sly smile, flashing happiness.

"It usually takes him a little while to warm up to me," Wendy says. "If you have any questions about what I'm doing, just ask."

She rolls a huge blue ball, about three feet in diameter, into the middle of the room. She puts Avery on top of the ball and holds him while she moves the ball around. He is forced to bring himself upright, to work his stomach muscles, by the movement of the ball. Avery is working hard and, every so often, he cries from the exertion. Wendy hands him to me and I comfort him, whispering to him, telling him how good he is doing. Next Wendy brings out a big purple dish filled with hundreds of tiny plastic balls and sets Avery inside. "This teaches him balance," she says, as Avery swims through the balls.

The half hour passes in a blink. "He's doing really well," Wendy says. "See you next week, Avery." He smiles again, shyly, and buries his head in my chest.

"Thanks for everything you're doing for him," I tell Wendy.

When I get him back to the car, Avery is already asleep.

The therapy sessions started two months ago on Friday afternoons. Then, two weeks ago, they were moved to Tuesday mornings. Jennifer and I forgot about the change and missed the last appointment. Wendy called to reschedule and Jennifer was in tears when she hung up the phone.

"It's only one appointment," I said, hugging her.

"You don't understand," she said. "This is the only thing I can do for Avery."

I tried my best to comfort Jennifer, telling her that one appointment wasn't going to make Avery crawl. But now, after going to the therapy session, I see how important it is to try to help him. I want him to learn how to crawl, how to stand and walk. I want him to know how to get back up if he gets knocked down in this life. He is my son. I am proud of him for doing his exercises, for trying his best. I drive through town, heading home. None of this is flashy or glamorous or anything I ever thought I'd be doing on a Tuesday morning. But the little kid in the backseat is my hero, my star, because he just keeps trying. It is the bravest thing in the world to do, just keep trying, one tiny step at a time.

One Good Horse

*   *   *

Driving home, on the highway in front of the colt's old pasture on the south shore of the lake, Bob passes me coming the other direction in his pickup truck, the trailer behind loaded with hay bales. I slow the car, pull into a driveway, and turn around, hoping that I can catch up to him in town. Bob pulls his truck and trailer into the parking lot of the hardware store and I park alongside. Avery is still asleep from his workout. I leave the car running and walk up to Bob, who is just now getting out of his truck. He is sweaty, little bits of hay sticking to his skin. He smiles when he sees me, and says, "You're missing out on all the fun."

"I thought you were going to call me to help you out."

"I would have called," he says, "but I had a little window of opportunity to get a load, so I jumped out it."

I point at the hay bales. "You've got to let me help you. Avery is with me right now, but if you park the trailer in the hay shed, I'll unload it tomorrow." I want the physical work, want the burn in my muscles and the satisfaction of doing work I can point to. And I want to repay Bob for boarding Blue. It will be good to have something waiting for me in the morning. I will get dressed and drive to Bob's place with something to do when I get there.

In the morning, I drink my coffee and get dressed and kiss Jennifer and the boys good-bye. When I drive down to the barn, I see the empty trailer, the hay already stacked in the shed.

Two N Bar herds are moving up the trail from Texas, going three hundred miles father north than where Teddy is now. He knows he is trading his more prestigious job as a rep for the dust and danger of the trail, but he can't help himself. He needs to go. He'll cross the Yellowstone, travel through the Big Dry country, to the mouth of the Musselshell, where it empties into the Missouri. A place on the map as a place in your life.

Teddy rides a hundred miles south and meets the herds on the Powder River at Cache Creek. One of the herds is led by Burgess, the other by Bowen, both Johns. Ten days later, just outside Miles City, they face the rushing waters of the Yellowstone. The ferry will shuttle the wagons across, but the twenty cowboys, one hundred and fifty horses, and four thousand steers will have to swim. On the near shore, Teddy takes off his clothes and puts them on the ferry. The others look at him like he'd been drinking, but he knows what he's about.

This is the Yellowstone, a hundred times more treacherous than the Red. Teddy rides naked, unshucked, the wind cutting his skin. He is on Jesse, a tall horse from Oregon, an animal accustomed to cold northern waters. They ride into the river, an icy blue flood of cowhide and cussing. The cowboys from Texas and their little cow ponies try to keep their positions, try to keep the cattle from milling and turning the crossing into a nightmare. The water is colder and faster than anything they've ever seen. One man jumps off his horse at the first icy slap of water, then grabs a steer's tail and lets it drag him across. Hooves and horseshoes paw for bottom. Teddy has that solid feeling again, the feeling that, though he knows it's not possible, he has been preparing for this crossing all his life.

On the far side, the other men shiver in their soggy clothes. They pour water out of their boots and wring out their socks. Teddy unpacks his dry clothes. He doesn't say a word, just smiles and hums a little as he gets dressed. The man they call Cow wonders aloud, "How far is it up no'th?" A direction as a place. A place, as a life.

As the day heats, the breeze moves up from the lake, bringing the smells of fish, the exhaust from the two-stroke engines of boats, and rubber against asphalt on the highway. And the highway brings the other man, the one who drives the white truck. He is the one with the rope and halter, the one with the brush. He picks up the colt's front hooves and cleans them with a pick, but when he tries to do the same with the rear hooves, the colt will not let him. The man smells of coffee and cologne. When he finishes cleaning the stalls in the barn, the man carries the scent of sawdust and manure and sweat. He starts the little cart and drives out into the field, manure flung from the machine. He fills the colt's water dish, stares at the animal for a while, before getting back in his truck and leaving the afternoon empty and warm.

Fred is in the barn, nailing trim along the floor of the tack room.

"Hi," I say. He nods and smiles, nails between his lips.

Little Leroy and his mother have been turned out into the arena now, so I decide to clean their stall. I strip the stall down to the bare dirt, wheelbarrow after wheelbarrow full of sawdust. I tell myself that I need to do this work to pay back Bob for boarding Blue.

The days are slipping by. Three kids can be a lot for one person to handle, so Jennifer and I usually split them up. I watch the babies while Carter has his piano lessons. I watch Carter and Bennett while Jennifer takes Avery to physical therapy. I bring Carter to the ranch to get him out of the house sometimes, but that means I can't work like I would if I were by myself. It's always something, and I haven't done nearly enough work for Bob, and I haven't worked with Blue as much as I've wanted to.

When I am finished, I stand in the doorway to the office drinking a bottle of water. I am stalling and I don't know why. Fred is here, if I happen to get hurt. The wind isn't blowing. It's not raining. The small pen is there, waiting. I need to ride my horse. I am out of excuses.

★　　★　　★

The man halters the colt, then brushes him down, talking softly. The saddle pad, then the saddle. Next comes the bit, which tastes bitter and metallic in the colt's mouth. The man leads the colt to the small round pen and closes the gate behind.

The man drapes the reins across the horse's neck. He

tightens the saddle's cinch. The colt takes a step back at the pull against his belly. The man steps into the stirrup, letting the colt feel his weight. The colt adjusts. The man lies across the saddle, waiting. The colt waits, too. The man swings his leg up and over the cantle of the saddle. The colt's muscles quiver at the full weight of the man. He turns his head around to nose the man's left boot. Time ticks by. There is the sound of the carpenter's hammer echoing from the barn. There is a breeze off the lake. Flies buzz around the colt. He switches his tail, stamps his back feet.

The man makes a clicking noise with his mouth. The colt pricks up his ears, but stands still. The man makes the noise again, this time kicking the colt gently in the flanks. The colt takes one step forward, still bothered by the flies.

The man swings down from the saddle. He hugs the colt around the neck, speaking softly, quietly. The flies are still bothering the colt. He stomps one time, then again. The man takes off the saddle, then the pad. There is a small stain of sweat where the weight of the man bore down on the colt's back. The breeze feels good across it.

The man feeds the colt grain, but no hay. When the young horse licks the last of the sweet feed from the rubber dish, the man opens the gate to the pen. The colt stands there, looking from the opening to the man and back. Finally, the horse takes a step forward, and then another, until he is outside the pen. He puts his head down and bites at a clump of grass, then lifts his head and watches the man walk back to his truck.

The house is empty when I get home from the ranch. Jennifer has left me a note telling me she's gone to the grocery store. *Brave woman,* I think, imagining her pushing one shopping cart full of kids, another piled with diapers and cartons of organic milk. But I've known all along that my wife is a brave woman. Tomorrow we will have been married a dozen years.

I plop on the couch and turn on the television. The Belmont Stakes is being televised. I'm not much on horse racing, but I'm intrigued by the spectacle of it all. It's still two hours before the ninety-second race is to begin, and the commentators are raving about a horse named Smarty Jones, a three-year-old that has raced eight times previously. If Smarty Jones can win this event, it will be the first time an undefeated horse has won the Triple Crown since Seattle Slew. After today, Smarty Jones will be retired. The sports commentators review how the horse spent the night, what time he woke up, what he ate for breakfast. And then there is a human interest segment in which schoolchildren are interviewed about the colt. They hold up crayon drawings of the horse and scream, "We love Smarty Jones!" He is a hero.

I think about Riskulus, Dr. Burnett's Thoroughbred stud, scratched from the Kentucky Derby seventy years ago. Brought to a remote island in northwest Montana to live out the rest of his days. I wonder if they share any blood, Riskulus and Smarty Jones and Blue.

When the race finally begins, a horse named Birdstone

comes from behind in the final stretch and beats Smarty Jones. An interviewer on horseback trots beside the winning jockey, asking him how it feels, and the jockey is almost sad to have won, with his broken English and mixed feelings.

Blue took only one step forward today, but I cheer him all the same. It was a huge victory. Afterward, I turned him out to pasture because with our wedding anniversary tomorrow and Avery and Bennett's birthday two days later, I don't know when I'll be out to visit him next, and I don't want Bob to have to cover for me. I'm sure Blue will be fine with the rest of the herd.

Out the window, I see Jennifer turn in our driveway and gun the car up the hill to our house. I click off the television, put on my shoes, and go out to help her.

The two herds move north, four days apart, to the place where the Musselshell River meets the Missouri. Teddy is with the first bunch, led by John Burgess, who is a few years older than Teddy. Burgess's mustache looks like a hairy brown bird, wings extended, perched on his upper lip. It flaps in the wind.

Nado, the old French trapper, rides ahead, scouting watering holes. There are no running streams, no rivers, in this dry land. Nado rides back to the herd, motioning to the northeast. *"Grand cour d'eau,"* he says proudly. *Gran-cor-dough.* It is nothing more than a greasy mud hole, large enough for an antelope or two to sip from, but Burgess knows his business. He cuts off a dozen steers at a time and lets them drink their fill, making sure none ever get thirsty enough to start a run.

When they finally make the Musselshell, the lead steers do run, but it is because they smell something dead near the grove of cottonwoods by the river. The men get the herd turned easily, but there is something eerie about the place. They turn the steers onto grass along the river, and go to work building corrals near the old fort. The other herd, the one led by John Bowen, gets caught in an early blizzard, and the Texas cowboys nearly freeze in place, the wind howling through them. When the work is finally done, Harry Rutter is left to look after things, while the rest of the men return to Miles City. Five men, including Teddy, will stay on with the outfit. He is promised only room and board through the winter, and a job that pays forty dollars a month when spring arrives. When they reach Miles City, the other fifteen men bypass the saloons and sporting houses and head for the depot, where they wait for the train that will take them back to Texas, and warmth.

In a month, Teddy will be twenty-four. He celebrates early and often.

We wear gold crowns made of cardboard. Avery and Bennett, sitting in their high chairs, smear frosting and ice cream into their hair. We sing along to the loud, goofy music on the stereo. Later, we play a spirited game of pin the tail on the donkey, sticking a yarn tail to a cardboard animal like pinning dreams on a life. I'm blindfolded, holding Avery in my arms, holding his tiny hand with the tail in it. Bennett squeals with glee. Then it is his turn with Jennifer. Then Carter.

We've come so far in the last year. Bennett has four teeth on top and four on the bottom. He knows how to say "Mom, Dad, Carter, All Done, I did it. Uh-oh." With him, it is all about numbers. The number of words he knows, the number of teeth he has, how much weight he's gained. He walks while pushing something in front of him, a wagon or a chair or a pet. He commands attention, always reaching for something. His pale blue eyes. He looks so much like Carter, when Carter was a baby, it is hard to tell them apart in photographs.

And then there's Avery. He has no teeth. He cannot walk. He cannot crawl. He cannot even really sit up without being supported. He is as weightless as a stuffed animal. He has no words. He coos and purrs and laughs. His belly, distended. He claps with one hand, holding it above his head, leaning back and watching it, listening, like he is waving good-bye to himself. Sometimes we call him "the Buddha." His disappearing smile. This uncarved block. This question mark. His everything. His nothing.

But this is not a time to add up all of the differences between the boys, it is a time to celebrate what each has in his own way.

Carter blows out the candles on the cupcakes for his little brothers. I make my own wish. Avery and Bennett haven't gotten much patience or understanding on my part in the last year. Unlike when Carter was a baby, all I want is for Avery and Bennett to grow up and get it over with. I'm afraid that I will look back and wish I had savored this time, instead of rushing things along, wanting them to grow up so that I might get on with my own life. They are my life, and I hope I can do better.

Carter licks the frosting from a cupcake and hands it to me. "Thanks," I say. He does the same with another cupcake and gives it to me. "I've already got one without frosting," I say.

"That one is for Blue," Carter says, "since he couldn't come to the party."

I don't see any of the horses when I drive down the hill to the barn. On the nightstand outside the office is the copy of Teddy Blue Abbott's book, *We Pointed Them North,* that I gave to Bob. There is a piece of yellow paper stuck to the cover and Bob has written "Thanks! This was a good one." I wanted him to keep this book, but it is too hard to explain in a message scribbled on the board, so I take the book and put it back in my truck. I grab the baggie from the front seat, then go back to the barn for a halter and rope, and I walk.

I pick my way up the hill, sidestepping stumps from the logging operation that thinned the timber on Bob's place. I think about the things we give people, and the things we take. Before Carter, I was terrified of little kids. Anytime a child approached me, I'd freeze up, scared that they'd ask me a question I couldn't answer, not knowing how to interact with them. Jennifer would tell me, "Just treat them like they are little people. Be normal, act decent, don't give them things they don't want." And it got easier.

I've always been the same way around people with disabilities. It's like I want to help them, when they aren't asking for help. I want to do something to fix their lives. But, since I can't, I end up avoiding them. There is a thrift store in a town to the north of us, which is run by and for disabled people. There is man with Down syndrome who works in the store. Every time I've been in the store with Jennifer, this man inevitably walks up to her and announces, "It's my birthday." Jennifer congratulates him, sometimes she gives him a hug. I dodge the man, heading to the book section when I see him coming down the men's clothing aisle with a pair of jeans on a hanger. At least one day a year, it is the man's birthday. Or maybe, he is reborn each gray morning. I promise myself next time Jennifer goes to the thrift store, I will go with her. I won't try to solve the man's problems, won't imagine he has any to solve, but I will shake his hand and say, simply, "Happy birthday."

The weeds are coming on strong in this pasture. Mostly, it is knapweed, a noxious plant that has beautiful purple flowers. It is nearly impossible to kill. There is hound's-tongue, with its small burrs later in the year, and burdock plants. I'll have to start spraying soon. Up ahead, I see Jesus, grazing alongside Mary and Pete, the black team. There is the donkey. And finally, Blue. He picks his head up as I approach, turns to face me. I scratch his neck, then open the baggie and hold the cupcake out to him. He sniffs it, then eats it in one swallow.

We've come so far, all of us, in the past year. I need to remember that my family is not an island. We really are a part of the whole. I think about the killdeer running down the road ahead of my truck, thinking how brave it was that he would lay down his life for his family, protecting them. I now see that the silly bird is putting on an act long after the danger is past. He just needs to fly.

I rub Blue on his withers, finding just the right spot and tell him, "Happy birthday to all of us," then walk back down the hill to my truck.

★　　★　　★

Winter on the Musselshell. It's just Teddy and Harry Rutter and the horse wrangler in the cabin they have fixed up. John Bowen, the trail boss, is forty-five miles away, in Rocky Point, watching that end of the range. There isn't much for Teddy to do but wait for spring. It's barely daylight at eight in the morning and the sun sets before five at night. The days drag on. Teddy sings and sings, his voice filling the tiny cabin, until Rutter rolls over on his cot and says, "Hobble yer lip." They don't speak after that.

The men ride out into the winter day and shoot deer for meat. They wait for grub-line riders to stop and visit, the lonely drifters thankful for a warm meal of venison and a place to bed down. And Teddy and Harry are grateful for the company. One man tells them about the vigilantes that worked that part of the country, hanging horse thieves and cattle rustlers. He points to the west wall of the cabin with his fork and says, "There's five buried there under that grove of cottonwoods by the mouth of the river."

Teddy looks over to Harry Rutter, both realizing that the smell of the dead men is what frightened the steers when they first arrived in that country. But they still aren't talking to each other. They look away.

Teddy knew all about the vigilantes. They were led by Granville Stuart, the first man to find gold in Montana, in 1858, now a partner in the DHS Ranch to the south. Teddy's heard that Stuart is different from most of the other ranchers in that he believes hired men should be able to have their own cattle and run them with their boss's herd. Another grub-line rider visits and tells the men that Stuart has two grown daughters living on the DHS. "They say he's offering five hundred head of cattle to the first man that'll marry the oldest one, but the younger one is finer than cream gravy." The men are silent, each considering their options, which are none except to get through the solitude and snow without killing one another.

That March, Burgess rides down and tells Teddy they are going to fence off some of the bottomland between the Missouri and the Musselshell for a hay field. He hands Teddy a grub hoe and points out where the fence should go. "I'll be back with a wagonload of posts and wire in a few weeks."

Teddy picks up a hoe and starts digging postholes. He knows about loyalty to an outfit. But he also knows that hay fields mean farming, and fencing is nothing he wants any part of. He needs to start building something bigger than what he has, more than what can fit on the back of his saddle.

When Burgess returns with the wagon a few weeks later, he can hardly find the postholes that Teddy dug. They are just shallow depressions in the dirt which have been filled back in from the spring rain. He looks to Teddy and tilts his head south. Teddy nods. His things are already packed.

It's the last week in June. For the past five days I've been taking up the old cross fence in the upper pasture, the same barbed wire the stud cut himself on when he went on his tear. Pulling up steel posts and rolling the barbed wire into rusty wreaths. I have to get this work done now, while the weather is decent. Once winter hits, I won't be able to make the drive out here, and there won't be any work to do. I'm not sure what is going to happen with Blue.

I am planning to work on the fence again today, but the horses are standing around the barn when I pull up. Blue picks his head up at the sound of the truck, and he nickers when I get out. I get the halter from the barn. I am done cleaning stalls as an excuse not to ride, done stalling. It's time to ride the colt, one way or another. If it means getting thrown, there are worse things. I just need to move forward.

I am in the small round pen, saddling Blue, when a silver flatbed pickup pulls down the hill and parks beside the barn. An outline of mountains, like jagged barbed wire, is painted on the door of the truck. An old man gets out of the passenger's side. It's Forrest.

I feel better that there is someone around, in case I wreck. And I feel proud that he is here to witness my first real ride on Blue. A woman gets out from behind the wheel of the truck, and she walks to the barn with Forrest.

I turn the stirrup toward me and step into it, letting

Blue feel my weight. Then with the reins in my left hand, I swing up onto his back in one move. I lean over the saddle horn and pat Blue's neck, praising him for standing still while I mounted.

I have one rein in each hand, ready to pull him in circles if he starts running with me. I cluck to Blue and, when he doesn't move, I use my heels. He bunches up under me, but then takes a step forward and stops. I cluck to Blue again, then give him some heel. He takes two steps forward. We keep going like this until he is finally walking stiff-legged around the perimeter of the corral. Around and around we go, like goldfish in a bowl.

I stop Blue, then turn him to go the other way. He moves away from the panels and cuts across the middle of the corral, bucking a little. I pull his head up, my heart racing, and get him back against the panels. We walk clockwise around the pen. I have to point my left toe in, so it doesn't get hooked in the slats of the panels, and it throws me off balance a little, riding with my leg tucked in. The brown metal corral encloses us, defines our space. It is like the set to some grade school play, as we perform our nervous, awkward dance. It is an island we are trying to make our way around. It isn't a very pretty ride, but it is a real ride.

In the distance, the sun sparkles off the water a thousand times over. Cars and trucks zoom along the highway as fast as they can go. This is all right, this little thirty-foot circle of sand. The larger world can wait.

Over at the barn, Forrest and the woman are getting back into the truck.

"Whoa," I say, but Blue keeps walking. I pull back on the reins gently and he stops dead. I step down from the saddle, open the corral gate, and lead the colt over to where the truck has pulled up and stopped in front of the single-wire electric gate.

Forrest is out of the truck, unhooking the plastic gate handle.

"Hello, Mr. Davis."

He looks up at me, sideways under his hat. "Hi, Tom." His cane is hooked over his arm. "I brought my daughter out to look at Bob's stud." The woman in the truck waves. "How's that little colt doing?" And I think he means Blue, but then he nods to the arena, where Leroy and his mother stand, looking at us through the rails.

"Oh, I think he's doing better. He was sure running and kicking there when I first showed up this afternoon."

"Well, that's good."

I pat Blue on the neck and say, "Today was the first time I've ridden him."

He sizes up the colt. "He got some Thoroughbred in him?"

"I think so, and quarter horse."

He stands there, holding the black plastic gate handle, the electric wire snapping like a pacemaker, and I can't think of a thing to say. The flatbed Dodge idles. Blue swishes his tail.

"Well," I say. "It was good seeing you again."

The old man smiles his gap-toothed smile and nods. He drops the wire to the ground and, after the pickup drives across, he bends down and picks it up again. He hooks it up and shuffles to the waiting truck.

I lead the colt to the barn, unsaddle him, then turn him back into the pen and give him some sweet feed. I watch him eat the grain. Forrest Davis doesn't really care about my horse. He has his own horses to train, his own life to live. He doesn't care that today was the first time Blue's been ridden, doesn't care if he is Thoroughbred or quarter horse, gelding or mare. *Good for you, bud. Good luck and Godspeed.* This is my deal. I leave the gate to the pen open, so Blue can wander free once he is done eating.

I open the door to the office and turn the light on. There, on the wall, is a message board. A red rag, for erasing the marker, is taped to a string alongside. On the left side of the board there is a CHECKLIST with black lines underneath. Bob has written, WEEDS on the first line, FENCE on the second. And seventeen lines down, LOVE YOUR KIDS.

In the evening, the air currents push down from the mountains, carrying the smells of the woods. Coyotes, deer, and bear. A flock of blackbirds, dozens of them, wings overhead, flying north. Stray fireworks, shot off by Indian kids over in Elmo, flicker and die in the fading light.

Chapter Five

TOMORROW IS THE MOST IMPORTANT THING
IN LIFE.
COMES INTO US AT MIDNIGHT VERY CLEAN.
IT'S PERFECT WHEN IT ARRIVES AND IT PUTS
ITSELF IN OUR HANDS.
IT HOPES WE'VE LEARNT SOMETHING FROM
YESTERDAY.

—Inscription on JOHN WAYNE'S headstone

Jennifer pushes the double stroller around the corral, Avery and Bennett blinking in the sun. Carter sits on the big wagon, sipping a can of orange soda from the refrigerator in the office. He arranges the spent fireworks he's collected from the pasture. Red plastic tail fins, which he calls "propellers," blue nose cones, hollowed-out cardboard cylinders. The smell of gunpowder and horse shit and dust lingers on this late July day.

I want to share Blue with my family, to have them escape the walls of our house along with me. I know that Jennifer misses the ranch in Miles City more than I do. She was so good with the horses, Balty and Cagey, patient and kind. I want Carter and his brothers to know what it means to care for animals, to put your life in their hands. I wonder if we could do this again as a family. If we could live on a ranch and raise livestock. This is my way of trying it out, of imagining a new future for us.

I haul my gear out to where Blue is tied in the corral and get him saddled. We ride clockwise, then counterclockwise. We've begun working on neck reining. When I want Blue to turn left, I touch the right rein against his neck. He hasn't learned this cue yet, so I take the left rein and pull hard, forcing him around to the left. Blue has already learned so much. He comes to me when he sees me. He accepts the bit, the saddle pad, the saddle, evenly and quietly. When I say "Whoa," he stops right away, and when I cluck my tongue, he steps forward.

We circle clockwise, counterclockwise, whoa. Left neck rein, nothing, left pull. Then we start up again, this time counterclockwise. Blue's ears twitch, and for a moment, I think he's going to stop, but instead he turns into the middle of the sandy corral and ducks his head. I'm not sure what he is doing, what he is thinking, until he begins to pitch forward, then back, gently, slowly bucking. I shift with him, forward, back. There isn't much to it. I pick his head up with the reins and stop him with a "Whoa." I pat his neck, asking, "What's that about?" We start up again, walking around and around and around.

I don't bother scolding Blue for his bucking. It's hard to be mad at him when he has been so gentle with me. Training him has been so easy, such a pleasure. When I thought about getting a colt, I imagined the worst—resistance, bucking, sore muscles, maybe even broken bones. I thought I wanted that fight, thought I wanted to feel physical pain, to bleed. There are so many things that might have happened to me if the wrong horse had come along. I could have ended up in the hospital, or worse. But instead, I found Blue, who treated me kindly. He gave me what I needed, though I didn't know it at the time.

I dismount and walk Blue through the metal gate, then lead him outside the big round corral, to where Jennifer is standing. She rubs his nose, and the babies look up and smile. "I'll go unsaddle him and then we can head out," I say.

"Don't hurry," Jennifer says. "We're having fun."

Blue and I walk to the barn, where I strip off the saddle and pad and put them away. Then we walk back outside, where I take Blue's halter off. He is free to go, but he doesn't run off, as I've come to expect when I turn a horse loose. Instead, he walks cautiously over to where Jennifer stands next to the stroller. I see a tiny hand reach up toward the colt. Blue lowers his head and the little five-pointed star touches him.

The DHS is better than he imagined. The boss, Granville Stuart, treats his men well if they work hard. The food is good, canned tomatoes and fresh-baked bread every day. The men sleep in tents. The horses are solid. And there is the boss's daughter, Mary. Teddy can hardly look at her without blushing. When she's around, he can't speak, can't breathe. He feels ill, hot and cold at once. Besides that preacher's daughter back at the FUF, she is the first good girl he's known since coming north.

Teddy bides his time, trying to get in good with Mary's father and mother. He does the dishes. He washes his own clothes. He even milks the dairy cows. In the spring, he is back on the gather, repping for the DHS. Stuart sends him near and far. His job is to look out for the interests of the outfit. Teddy knows all the brands on the range, knows who will cheat you and who plays it straight. He works hard for his boss, trying to prove himself worthy. Teddy keeps his own counsel and keeps his nose clean.

Winter comes too soon. He rides with Pike Landusky, a powder keg on horseback just waiting for something to set him off. The old man hired him for his toughness. Six years ago, Landusky got in a shoot-out with some Blackfeet Indians. When he was finally found by a group of soldiers, Landusky had passed out, part of his jaw lying in the corner of the cabin. He had broken it off and thrown it there after getting shot in the face. The doctor in Lewistown had to reset the mangled jaw, Landusky croaking, "If I die, I die." He weighs two hundred pounds and stands over six feet tall. The slobber freezes on his reconstructed face in the bitter wind.

They wear all the clothes they have, two layers of long wool underwear, pants and overalls and chaps, two pairs of gloves and wool socks. Landusky is happy to be out in the blizzard, glad to be away from his mad French Canadian wife with her sharp tongue and their seven kids. He is smiling under the mask he has fashioned from the liner of a torn jacket, not to hide his tortured jaw, but to keep from going snow-blind in the never-ending white of the blizzard. Landusky thinks it is too cold for Indians or rustlers to be out stealing cattle, but he was hired to do the job, and that's what he's going to do. He stops, takes off his gloves and rolls a cigarette, pinching the loose tobacco from the pouch he made from the bladder of a Brule Sioux who stole a piece of buffalo meat from him years ago. He warms at the thought of it, and at the smoke he will soon hold in his lungs.

Teddy isn't nearly as cheerful. He has never felt cold like this. He thinks he might just break down and make a mask for his own face, to keep his eyeballs from falling out of his head at the whiteness and the cold. There are no rustlers stealing the DHS cattle, no Indians to fight. And the cattle, the smart ones, have made themselves scarce, hiding out of the wind, hunkering down in the draws and coulees between the Missouri and the Milk Rivers. Some drift to the banks of the rivers, and the ones in the back push the ones in front out onto the ice, toward the open water in the middle. Teddy wishes he was back at the DHS headquarters, back with Mary.

But instead they are out here, along the slopes of the Little Rockies, the last open range before Canada. It had been such a hot summer, the grass eaten down to nothing. Now Teddy and Landusky do what they can to push the cattle back into the hills, away from the icy waters.

The day before Christmas they break camp, load the old packhorse, and head south toward Landusky's cabin, where Rock Creek flows down out of the Little Rockies. They ride along the shoulder of the mountains, thinking of Christmas dinner and of the warmth of a stove. That night, Christmas Eve, a new wave of fresh snow crashes from the sky. Teddy and Landusky ride to Healy's ranch on Lodgepole Creek to get out of the blizzard. But the snow stretches on into the night, and the next day, Christmas, and the next, before they can finally venture out, their horses plunging through the chest-high drifts, the air like breathing the shattered blue glass of a broken medicine bottle, the horses eating pine needles to stay alive.

They push cattle back into the hills, the ones that are still able to move. The weather breaks for a little bit, just enough to melt the snow, before the temperature plummets again, forming a hard crust of ice atop the snow. The cattle can't paw through it to what little grass lies below. Their feet and hooves are scraped raw. Teddy writes his boss a note, telling the old man it's bad. He can only hope that there will be enough cattle left in the spring that he can still be a cowboy, that every last bovine isn't going to die.

At the end of March, Teddy sheds his crazy winter clothes and the face mask. Old Man Stuart figures many of his cattle have drifted south, so he sends Teddy and some others after them. Teddy takes one last pinch of tobacco from Landusky's pouch and rolls a cigarette and heads out. He makes a big swing down and finds only a lone steer who won't budge. The slat-ribbed steer just stares at the man on horseback with a sort of resigned hate. The other cattle are dead, piled in the draws where they sought shelter until they froze. Of the forty thousand head the DHS inventoried the previous fall, only seven thousand cattle survive. It is the end of so many things.

One Good Horse

I drive the Gator up the hillside, dodging stumps, to the fence that looks like it begins in the middle of the pasture, which is as far as I've come in taking it down. I park, take my pink plastic bucket and fencing pliers from the back, and start working on the top wire. I walk from post to post, removing the metal clip that holds the top wire and dropping it into the bucket. I do this ten times, set the bucket on the ground, then cut the top wire with the wire cutters on the pliers and roll the wire into a two-foot roll. By the time I am back where I started, I have a rusty wreath of barbed wire, which I tie off and put into the back of the six-wheeler. Then I start on the second wire, dropping clips into the bucket. Then the next wire, and the next. Finally there are ten bare steel posts in the ground. I get the post jack from the back of the six-wheeler and walk to the first post and ratchet it out of the ground. The hard work feels good, and its result—the land cleared of this dangerous old fence, the pasture made whole—feels even better. The only problem is that since I've been working on the fence, I haven't spent any time with Blue. When he was in the corrals, I had to feed him and clean his pen each day. Now that he is out on pasture, I am lucky if I catch a glimpse of him walking through the woods while I work. I don't want him to sour on me from not being ridden, to spoil from neglect.

I don't know what is going to happen to Blue this winter. I've heard Bob say time and again that he is grass-poor. Blue is one more mouth to feed. Bob has already rounded up the goats and taken them away. They were supposed to eat the noxious weeds that choke out the pasture grass, but they chose instead to squeak under the fence and lie on the haystack. Once I get done with the fence, I plan to start spraying knapweed, but it might be too late. I am afraid that me and Blue are next in line to go. My biggest fear is that Bob will ask me what my plans are for Blue. I don't have an answer.

He milks the Brown Swiss, warm streams hitting the sides of the pail. One, two, one, two. He never thought he'd ever be milking cows for a living. Spading potatoes from the garden like some farmer. But it's what he's come to in this life. The boardinghouse pays twenty cents a gallon for the milk and a penny a potato. The mines in Gilt Edge are booming, and the miners at the boardinghouse can't get enough food. Twelve saloons, a jail, a hotel, and sixteen hundred people working the hills. The Brown Swiss coughs up her cud and chews lazily.

Teddy is thirty years old.

He quit the DHS when Granville Stuart hired that new foreman, the one Teddy swore he'd never work for. By then, he'd already proposed to Mary. They were picking berries along the river when he took her hand in his and asked if she'd do him the honor. That shy smile and those big brown eyes, her nod, and his life was forever changed. He gave up chewing tobacco. Gave up whiskey. And he knew he had to give up cowboying, too, if he was to live up to the expectations he had for himself as a husband and a father. The cowboy life was for single men, for loners. Old man Stuart, his future father-in-law, didn't care that Teddy was quitting. After that bad winter, he'd lost so much his heart wasn't in it any longer. He was making plans to sell out.

Teddy went to work for the PW, the big horse outfit on Musselshell. Twelve hundred horses and a handful of cattle. Soon after, Mary's mother delivered her last baby and contracted a fever. She died two weeks later. Katie, Mary's older sister, caught consumption and died too. Teddy and Mary put off the wedding, unable to celebrate with so much tragedy around them.

He started working in the mine at Maiden, pushing an ore car underground until he forgot what the sun looked like. The headaches from the blasting powder were so bad, he couldn't even see. But he did it for her, for Mary. He wanted to make her proud. To save money so they could start their life together.

September 29, 1889, almost two full years after they were engaged, Teddy and Mary stood in front of the justice of the peace in the little town of Alpine. They pledged their love to each other, in sickness and in health, until they were dead, and beyond. She wore a red velvet dress that she had made especially for the day. He wore his best white shirt, his heart bleeding through it. They rented a little house outside Gilt Edge. He planted a big garden, bought a few cows to milk. That was a year ago.

Mary is in the house now, fixing dinner, a baby on her hip and another on the way. He strips the last of the milk from the cows teats, then turns her out with the others.

His arm is sore, a reminder of the wreck he had when he saved Bill Charlton all those years ago. He takes the pitchfork and throws some hay into the pen for Little Billy, still the most honest horse he ever knew. He takes the pails of milk to the springhouse and pours them into the jug that is cooling there. And then he walks back to the house in the dark of night, hearing the wind singing through the wires of the fence all around, the baby crying. He closes the white wooden gate behind him and heads up the steps into the house.

Sometimes walking in circles is the only thing that will calm Bennett. If he is crying, I whisper to him as we walk, telling him all of the things that happened that day, or listing the many wonders he might see in his life, if only he'll stop crying and go to sleep. When I whisper, he quiets himself and tries to listen. Walking these nights away with Bennett reminds me of the times I'd ridden Blue around the corral, clockwise, counterclockwise, around and around and around.

Out the living room window, the sun is just setting over the mountains to the west, blanketing everything with a glow in a way that you can't paint or photograph or explain. I stop to watch the light shift and change, but Bennett stirs and cries out. So I walk. An hour before midnight, the sky still holds the last of the day's dying light. It's just a seam above the hills to the west, a thin line separating hills and clouds, today from tomorrow. I walk

Bennett around and around, trying to get him to sleep. Finally I lie down on the couch with him in my arms.

It is the dead of night. My fire department pager is going off, shrieking an alarm. The county dispatcher's voice paging out a mutual aid request from the fire department in town. A deck on a local bar has collapsed. When the tones sound on the pager, it opens up to all radio traffic. Bennett asleep on my chest, I listen to the sounds of the incident. The parking lot of the bar is so crowded, the fire trucks can't get close to the building. They need floodlights. They need more help. When the fire chief calls for more ambulances, I can hear people screaming in the background. He calls for a dozen ambulances, two helicopters. I take Bennett to his crib and lay him down, get dressed, and take off, hoping the noise of my truck doesn't wake my sleeping family.

By the time I am halfway to the fire hall, the big fire engine has left the station with five on board. Unless the chief in town calls for more help, there is no point in going any farther. Too late, again, to do anything heroic, I turn around and head home to listen to the radio. They are triaging patients at the scene, taking the most seriously hurt first. The rest follow. In all, seventy people are shuttled to the hospital in the next hour. In another hour, the radio goes quiet, the whole thing is over.

The old man's memory races from one thing to the next. He wants to get it all down, wants to get it right. The pretty young woman from back east sits across from him, her slender hand holding a pen poised over a pad of paper. Her name is Helena, like the town two hundred miles to the west.

He has told her about how he met Charlie Russell on the DHS gather in the spring of '86, just before that bad winter. How Charlie was working for the OH Ranch that winter and how, instead of trying to use words to tell the absentee bosses back in Helena how grim the situation was, Charlie painted a little watercolor, no bigger than a postcard. It showed a ganted-up longhorn, all ribs and horns, coyotes and hawks impatient on the edges, waiting for the steer to take its last breath. It was called *Waiting for a Chinook or The Last of Five Thousand*. The little watercolor made Charlie Russell famous. And, over the years, Charlie and Teddy stayed in touch, two old cowboys who remembered the open range and the way things used to be. Teddy tells the girl how, just a few years ago, he had to sell some of the illustrated letters Charlie had sent to him, the ones with little sketches on the envelopes. It broke his heart to part with old Charlie's letters, but his family was hungry and Teddy needed the money. He tried to sell his stories about the West, too, about what it was like bringing those longhorns up the trail sixty years ago, but the magazines weren't interested in the truth. They wanted shootouts, wanted action.

He clears his throat and starts into the songs they used to sing while on night guard. "The Little Black Bull," "The Cowboy's Lament," "The Ogallaly Song," his once strong voice settling like dust in the air of the little farmhouse.

Mary is in the other room making lunch. Next September, they will have been married fifty years, and they will have a party. Mary will wear the same beaded red dress she wore on their wedding day. He doesn't tell the girl this, but when Mary goes to town, he takes out the little satchel he keeps hidden away, undoes the rawhide tie that secures it, and pulls out the things he has saved. A few of his favorite letters from Charlie Russell, the ones he couldn't part with. The silver ring from the Seventh Cavalry given to him by that Indian so long ago. And the letters Mary has written to him through the years, her words coming to him across time.

The girl asks him how he feels about giving up the life of a cowboy, the drinking and chewing tobacco, the horses and wagons. He doesn't have an answer. But he knows he came out on the good end of things, knows that he got back more than he should have from this life. Five sons, three daughters. The 3-Deuce Ranch built up to two thousand acres, fifty thousand dollars in the bank at one time.

Mary is calling them to lunch.

After, the girl drives them out to the old fort in her rented car. It's just a mile from where the DHS ranch house once stood, where he first met Mary. Teddy gets out and walks around, kicking at rusty cans, picking nails from the dirt. He finds the cemetery and points to the headstones, there's the Foley boy, there's the Duffy baby. Those wooden markers, the ones over there, are Mary's sisters, Lizzie and Kate, and their mother, Aubony. The empty spots belong to nine soldiers dug up and reburied with Custer at Little

Bighorn. There is so much to remember, and Teddy is getting tired. They climb back into the car and the girl drives them back to the little farmhouse outside Gilt Edge, the town itself nothing but ghosts now.

It is the second day of April when an advance copy of the book arrives, but by then, Teddy is too sick to read it. It's in his lungs. His daughter, Mary, puts the book on the nightstand next to his bed. Five days later, on Good Friday, Teddy Blue is gone.

Mary and the children bury him in the tiny cemetery at Fort Maginnis. They choose a headstone for him and have it engraved with the epitaph he has requested:

EDWARD C. "TEDDY BLUE" ABBOTT
BORN DECEMBER 1860
DIED APRIL 1939
FATHER

Carter and I walk, hand in hand, through the summer grass in the lower pasture. Hoppers jump ahead of our footsteps. "There's a rock you missed," Carter says, pointing to a huge boulder.

"Yeah," I say, "I missed a lot of them." I could spend a lifetime picking rocks from the field and never make a dent in it. Carter and I kick through the grass until we find what we've been looking for. It's the tailpiece to another spent firework. Now Carter can occupy himself playing rockets while I work with Blue.

We ride around and around, work on neck reining and

turning, "go" and "whoa." Then we reverse directions and go the other way an equal number of times, the minutes winding and unwinding. I dismount, open the corral's large wooden gate, and hold a finger to my lips, signaling to Carter to stay quiet.

I swing back into the saddle and bring Blue around the corral one last time, then point him toward the open gate. Blue hesitates, then ducks his head and walks through. Bob's Oberlanders graze a few yards away across the electric wire, but Blue doesn't pay them any attention. Little Leroy and his mother. Jesus and the donkey. We pass them all, heading out of the little corral, then the larger one, riding out into the wide world. Blue doesn't need the boundaries of rails or fence to keep him under me. I finally feel as if I've accomplished something. We turn left toward the big lake, and the open country beyond.

Teddy Blue had no parting words for me. I was grateful that Helena Huntington Smith had captured the old man's story before it died with him, but the book ended with him talking about the songs he sang on the trail, and I was disappointed. Then there's Forrest Davis, another man I thought might have a lot to teach me. I think about Bob saying he is going to lock Forrest in a room with a tape recorder to get it all down before the old man dies, but I don't see it happening. I'm afraid one day I'll ask Bob how Forrest is doing and he'll shake his head and bite his lip at a loss for words. But maybe it will work out. Bob once said that Forrest will outlive all of us.

The old fence is finally gone, reduced to a pile of coiled

wire and a stack of steel posts alongside the little shop up near Bob's house. I've sprayed weeds and gotten sick on the chemicals when the wind changes and drifts back on me. I've cut and split firewood for Bob's woodstove. I've done everything I can think of, mostly to avoid thinking about the end of summer. I don't know where Blue will go when the snow falls and Bob has to start feeding hay.

And I don't know what my future holds. I want to be on a real cattle ranch again, to find a place where I can give myself over to the work. I don't know how to do that here, in this place of golf course developments and vacationers and twenty-acre parcels. We could take Blue to a working cattle ranch and finish training him there, turn him into an honest-to-goodness cow horse, have him be a part of all our days, mine, Jennifer's, the boys'.

Or I could train Blue until he is solid, then donate him to a riding therapy program. Kids with learning disabilities or physical handicaps could ride, and Blue could give them the chance to become bigger, stronger, faster than they are used to being, to see the world in a new way.

Or I can continue to stumble along.

What I don't want is for Blue to languish, to become some never-used, seldom-thought-of pet, a Western lawn ornament decorating the scene in someone's vacation photos. Blue deserves better than that. But I don't know what's next for the two of us, so I keep waiting, hoping that some answer will make itself clear. I should talk to Jennifer about it, but she has her hands full with the children. I should find Bob and talk to him, but I don't know how to even begin the conversation.

*   *   *

When I pull down to the barn, Bob is there. Two Oberlanders are tied to his yellow trailer.

"Thought I'd hitch up a team and see what sort of wreck I can get into," Bob says, smiling. "You want to learn how to drive?"

"Sure," I say, though I've never really considered it before. I inherited a nervous gene, something inside of me that imagines the worst. I picture myself tangled in a mess of reins, bouncing on the seat of a runaway wagon, looking for something solid to run into while the team runs out of control and Bob lies broken in the dust.

Bob goes through all of the equipment, telling me the names of the various pieces of the driving harness as he hitches up Digger and Nuff, the leather that goes over a horse's head and rests on his neck, the overcheck and the crupper. The leather reins are called lines. I keep waiting for the right moment to steer the conversation around to the coming winter, but there are so many buckles and adjustments to be made, and Bob is talking quickly, and I become lost just trying to take it all in. Before I know it, Bob is saying, "Help me roll the wagon up behind the horses, and then we'll be close to heading out."

I push the big rectangular wagon from the back, while Bob pulls from the front and steers the tongue between the two horses. He attaches chains and hooks and we're ready to go.

Bob climbs up into the seat and takes the four lines in his hands. "Go ahead and untie Digger's lead rope, then walk around and do the same with Nuff." I move cautiously, but quickly. Bob says, "Digger, Nuff, baaaack," and the wagon moves backward with the big horses. "Jump on up here," Bob tells me.

I climb onto the wagon from the back ladder and walk up to the front bench.

"You always want to call out to the horses by name, then tell them what you want them to do," Bob says. Then, in a firmer voice, he yells, "Digger, Nuff, haw." The horses turn left in unison and the wagon rolls smoothly behind them. "Haw means left and gee means right," Bob tells me, and then he hands me the lines.

I put my feet up on the wagon, like Bob's, and concentrate on the lines. The ones in my left hand go to the left side of each horse's bit, and the ones in my right hand go to the right. My stomach is burning. I wish I had some antacids. The wagon is barely moving and we are already going too fast for me. I wish I'd told Bob about my nervous gene. We go down a straight stretch of dirt by the barn, and we begin to pick up speed. I panic. "Whoa," I yell, checking the horses with the lines.

"Pull back and stop them now," Bob says. "And remember to use their names."

My mind blanks out. I can't remember the names.

"Digger, Nuff, whoa!" Bob calls out, reaching up and pulling back on the lines.

When the horses have stopped, Bob explains, "You meant to slow them but you said 'whoa,' which means stop. These guys need to know that stop means stop. Now, give them some slack and call them by name and tell them to walk."

I take a deep breath, thinking what a bad idea this is, but I don't want to disappoint Bob, and I think if I just stick with it, my nerves will settle. "Digger, Nuff, walk," I say.

The horses step out. The clatter of the harness, the rattle of the wagon's wheels. It feels way too powerful. I look over and Bob is sitting back, smiling, content, happy to be out here. It takes all of my concentration to make a small circuit around the corrals, and by then, my nerves are shot. My conversation with Bob about the future will have to wait for another day.

The pager goes off again in the middle of the night. It sounds like a routine "truck in the ditch" call—someone heading home from the bar fails to make a corner and ends up stuck. I gather my boots and jeans and dress in the living room, then start my truck and head out. About halfway to the fire hall, I hear our first-response engine call in that it's leaving the station with three people on board. A few minutes later, the other fire truck, the small one that I am a captain of, takes off with one on board. I drive to the fire hall anyway, the wind whipping the tree branches in my headlights. The first engine radios in that there is a pickup on the side of the road with damage to its front end. No one is around, but there is a dead horse in the ditch.

Pickup versus horse, most likely the collision of two unique Montana customs. Montana is still under open range law, which basically means that owners of livestock aren't necessarily liable for damage their animals cause. If you don't want a rancher's cows grazing your lawn, it is up to you to fence them out. And, for the time being, it's legal to drive with an open container of alcohol in your vehicle. As long as you aren't impaired beyond the legal limit, it's perfectly okay for you to drink and drive. It's not surprising to find out that Montana has the highest rate of alcohol-related fatalities in the United States.

I get to fire hall just as the first truck radios back. There isn't any gas or oil or coolant leaking from the truck, and the truck and horse are well off the road. There's nothing to do. They clear the scene and return to the hall.

When the smaller fire truck of the two comes back in, I see the spray of blood shotgunning its white paint. I try to scrub it off with a paper towel before it dries, but it is too late. I find a bottle of window cleaner and spray it on the blood, but it still won't come off. I don't want it there. The red is too much on the glossy white paint. I scrape and scrub until it is wiped clean, then toss the bloody towels in the trash can.

I drive home. Sometime in the night, Carter has moved into our bed, so I lie down in Carter's room, polar bear sheets and plastic lights in the shape of trout swimming above me, Carter's little boy smell still warm on his pillow.

I can't sleep. Before dawn, I slip out of the house and drive back to the highway and turn north. I don't know what I expect to see. Maybe if I could just see what color the horse is, it'd be enough, but when I get there, the horse is already gone. All that's left of him is a greasy blood stain on the pavement and a sad, solitary horse apple in the right-hand lane.

*   *   *

On a rainy day in the middle of September. Jennifer and I pack the kids into the car and drive south. It snowed up high last night, and fresh snow veils the Mission Mountains. Winter is coming, and I'm not sure where the time went.

We are heading south into Missoula, then down Reserve Street, past the strip of big box stores and fast-food restaurants. Past the turnoff to the hospital where the babies spent the first weeks of their new lives. Past the fairgrounds, on to Playfair Park. Midget football teams do warm-up exercises in the park's many fields, their bright solid jerseys the only spots of color in the morning drizzle. We pull in and Jennifer gets out to register us for the third annual Buddy Walk.

The sign-up table is beneath a shelter in the picnic area. We get five blue-and-yellow T-shirts, two adult sizes and three children's. Three balloons, two blues and a yellow. I disentangle the double stroller from the car while Jennifer puts the shirts over the boys' coats. First Bennett, then Avery into the stroller. They've been awakened from their naps and they are cranky. Jennifer pushes the stroller back and forth, back and forth, trying to soothe the babies. I'm doubtful about this whole day, but Jennifer said, "Just try it. We don't have to stay if we don't like it," so here we are.

There are one hundred and fifty Buddy Walks nationwide, held in an attempt to promote Down syndrome research, education, and awareness. The walk in Missoula was started by the McGowan family and their friends in honor of Danny, their two-year-old son with Down syndrome who died in a drowning accident. Before the walk begins, a kilted bagpipe player drones out the melody to "Danny Boy," and as the children pass him, they release their balloons. Carter and I watch his until it is just a blue dot in the gray sky and then it is gone altogether. At least we still have Avery to hold and to love. Putting on the Buddy Walk T-shirt, I become one of the team, something I never thought I'd be. I'm not a joiner. But I pull the shirt over my hooded sweatshirt and become a part of the event.

Three University of Montana football players carry a Buddy Walk banner and participants line out behind them. Almost immediately, the drizzle turns to rain. The walk is a mile around the park. We follow a course marked by yellow and blue balloons. The park is crowded with families, for the football games, for the walk. We all get wet together, all of us blessed by the cold rain.

I almost didn't come because I couldn't imagine it as anything other than a parade of hopelessness, me not being able to look people in the eye, wishing I wasn't there. But in the end, it is hard to tell the people who have Down syndrome from their parents, their friends, the other people at the park. The people with Down syndrome look like their families more than they look like one another, everyone wearing the T-shirts, wet faces bleeding into one another, blending together, in a parade where everybody is a hero. I'm glad we came.

I still haven't figured out where to winter Blue. I imagine renting a pontoon boat and pulling up to a dock in Big Arm in the middle of the night. I'll tie the boat and walk the rest of the way, keeping low and out of sight in the moonlight. Blue will nicker and come to me. I'll slip the halter over his nose, ride him bareback, race down to the water's edge. His hooves won't slip when he steps onto the artificial grass of the boat's deck. He'll bend his neck down to eat it, but will look up, goofy and confused.

It is a short trip, the motor purring in the night. Gravel scrapes the bottom of the boat, and I step onto the shore with Blue right behind. It will be something historic, mythical, the appearance of another horse, a spirit horse on Wildhorse Island. The colt carries no brand, no mark of ownership, just hooves and hide and heart. I'll take the halter off, hug him around the neck and kiss him on the nose. He'll stand there, watching me as I push the boat back into the water. And then he'll turn, smell the other horses, and run off to find them.

I drive to Bob's store on an October Sunday. Bob's Dodge is parked in the lot, the flatbed trailer hitched to the truck. A sign on the door of the store reads SORRY, WE'RE OPEN. Inside, a crowd of people listen to Bob as he plays his accordion and sings an old cowboy tune. I wander around looking at all the photographs on the walls, the old rodeo memorabilia. The music stops and the customers applaud.

I walk over to Bob. He is talking with an older couple. "I'll buy you and the missus lunch," he offers, "if you help us haul hay today." They decline, but decide to take him up on his offer of a discount if they sing "America the Beautiful" at the front cash register.

A few minutes later, we are in Bob's truck. He fiddles

with the tape player, trying to find a particular song. "Here it is," he says. It is an old-time Mexican cowboy song, sung in Spanish. "This is the best hay-hauling music." We listen as the truck flies south. I remember when Bob and I first came down this way to get the vaccinations for Blue. I remember how skinny the colt was, and what a big mistake I thought I'd made. He's grown into himself now, become a horse, but I'm still not sure if I made a mistake or not.

At Ronan we head west, out of town. We stop at the grain elevator and weigh the truck and empty trailer on the scale, then head back on the highway, west into the country, Bob trying to find the right section road to turn off on. We find it, and pull up to a huge stack of small square bales. Bob backs the trailer up to the hay and parks. There is another pickup there, its trailer already loaded with bales. "You know Ray Rose?" Bob asks.

"Yeah," I say. "What's he doing out this way?"

"This is part of his boss's operation," Bob says.

We walk over and help Ray tarp his hay, which he's going to haul to Idaho. While we're working, I ask Ray if he's seen my old boss lately.

"I saw Phil a week ago, I guess," Ray says.

"You know," I say, "I've been meaning to ask you something for the longest time. It's about that place your family used to own out on Eli Gap Road."

"Well, sure," Ray says, "what do you want to know?"

"My wife and I almost lived there when we first moved here. And then I was there when the fire department burned it down."

"Yeah?"

I want to ask him how he feels about the house he grew up in being gone now, but the best I come up with is "I was wondering how long you lived there."

"Oh, I never lived there," Ray answers. "Dad bought that place in '71 or '72. I grew up where I'm still living, right next door to my mom's place. Wait, I guess I did live there for a few months while I was going through my divorce. It was winter, and every morning I'd wake up and there'd be a drift of snow in front of the bedroom door, because it was so drafty. The chimney was always catching fire, too, and I was scared the place was going to burn down with me in it. All night long you could hear the mice carrying things off."

So I got it all wrong. I thought the vacant lot with its trio of apple trees was something that would make Ray sad. But he's probably happy he no longer has to look at the place, a reminder of his divorce, of cold winter nights.

"It was good seeing you again, Ray," I say.

"You too. I'll tell Phil you were asking after him." He gets in his truck and drives off.

It takes Bob and me about an hour to throw the bales down from the big stack and restack them on his trailer. Then we secure the load for the drive back to his ranch. Bob holds up a brand-new yellow strap, four inches wide, thirty feet long.

"I got a new strap," he says proudly, throwing it over the top of the stack. And then he laughs. "God, fifteen years ago I was in Switzerland singing Puccini, and now I'm happy just to have a new strap for hauling hay."

We weigh the loaded trailer at the elevator again, so he

can tell Ray how many tons of hay we took, and figure out what he owes. Then we stop at McDonald's for coffee. It costs a dollar twenty-five.

"I'll flip you for the quarter," Bob tells the teenaged kid behind the counter.

The kid looks confused. "Uh, okay," he finally says.

"Heads or tails?" Bob asks.

"Umm . . . tails?"

Bob tosses the quarter into the air and slaps it down on the counter. Heads. The kid doesn't know what to do. "Aw, don't worry about it," Bob tells him, handing him the quarter. "Don't want you to get in trouble over it." He winks.

We get back in the truck and head to the ranch, sipping hot coffee and listening to Bob's hay-hauling music as the landscape flies past. "We should take Judy Martz and some horses over to Miles City for the Bucking Horse Sale next spring," Bob says.

I'm confused. Judy Martz is the governor of Montana. "Why Judy?"

"That's the name of the wagon," Bob explains. "We can ride in the parade. You should think about it. Maybe we can ride in the sale too. You ride saddle broncs, right?"

Not really. I did it once, no, twice, in my life. But I nod yes. It'd be fun, going back to Teddy Blue's old town, to my old town.

"And you'll have to come up to Essex next New Year's," he says. "I do sleigh rides at the Izaak Walton Inn. If you help me with the horses we can get a room for your family and your wife and the kids can play in the snow." The same place where our family goes to eat for Mother's Day.

"Sure," I say, "that'd be fun."

Bob changes the tape in the player. "You know Harry Chapin?" he asks.

"Didn't he do 'Puff the Magic Dragon'?"

Bob just laughs and hits the PLAY button.

At the big red barn, we stack the hay. Dusty flakes of hay get under the back of my collar and itch, but it is good hard work. Soon the pile is stacked tight, with just two broken bales. Bob drives the truck through the lower pasture and I stand on the back of the trailer, kicking loose hay from the broken bales for the horses. Blue is there, one among the others. He looks like the horses in the photographs of the old days on the range, like a little cow pony, quick and strong. He looks beautifully at home here.

I tell Bob, "I think I'm going to turn my horse loose on Wild Horse Island." It is my way of opening the discussion about what's going to happen to Blue this winter. For once, Bob seems at a loss for words. He looks at me, mouth open, a piece of nicotine gum on the verge of falling out.

He recovers. "Well, maybe we can borrow Dave Mercer's houseboat, or maybe we can get Denny McCrumb to let us use his barge. Just be sure not to tell anyone that you're doing it." He winks. After a moment, he says, "I really appreciate all the work you've done around here. I'm a little afraid you've put in too many hours."

"Not at all," I say, thinking I haven't worked nearly enough.

"I don't want it to get in the way of our friendship," he

says. "I think you're being a little, what's the word . . ." He squints his eyes. "Nefarious. You're being a little nefarious with your hours."

I laugh.

"Well, I do know one thing. You don't need to worry about buying your horse any hay this winter. We'll have plenty."

Friendship. Plenty.

It's all I need. My colt has a home, at least for a while. And Bob considers me a friend.

Imagine horses grazing in autumn's failing, falling light. The huge honey-colored mares, pregnant with foals that will be born next spring, pick at the cured grass. A squat donkey rubs his haunches against a Ponderosa pine. A colt stands alone, just over there. He has grown into himself, his muscles becoming thick from a summer spent running up and down the gentle hillside above the lake. His coat is dark brown, lightening near his muzzle and eyes. There is a band of white above his right rear hoof, and a patch of white hair near his left wither, as if a bird has been perching there. His hooves are sound, his tail is long and silky. A faint star of white hair shines on his forehead. At the sound of an approaching truck, he lifts his head and picks his way, graceful and sure-footed, down the hill toward the barn.

Imagine. The team is harnessed and hitched to the wagon. Digger and Nuff stamp their hooves impatiently. I go to the barn for a halter and see the old man slumped in the sky blue recliner. I lift his weightless body and carry him to the wagon. Bob is there, motioning for me to take up the lines. And I do. I am not nervous anymore. I cluck my tongue, call the team by name, and we head out, the brown colt following behind. As the wagon rumbles down the gravel road, a killdeer takes flight. Silhouettes filter out of the timber and fall into line. Jennifer's father is there, a drink in one hand and barbecue tongs in the other, and he is humming "Unchained Melody." Tim, my former boss, trots up on the horse he calls Rip. He is older now, as we all are. Phil rides Dipper and Ray Rose is there on Draco, the stumblebum. The cowboy I bought the colt from is there, his eight sons fanned out behind, riding wild-eyed two-year-olds. At the highway, fire trucks gleam pure white and red in the moonlight. The endless parade, all of us, rallying to the sound of one tiny hand clapping.

We march across the Montana landscape, towards Gilt Edge and beyond, to the cemetery at Fort Maginnis. A fireman takes bolt cutters and snips the fence that surrounds it. Range cattle wander in, and the old cowboys buried beneath can once again feel the pulse of the hooves over their hearts. We circle the cemetery. It doesn't take long to find him, a headstone that reads:

EDWARD C. "TEDDY BLUE" ABBOTT
BORN DECEMBER 1860
DIED APRIL 1939
FATHER

Father.

That one word telling me everything I've been looking for all along. In the end, it is all I am. It is all that I need to be. It was there all along, and I missed it. Sometimes a line in a story or a shaft of sunshine over the landscape can become so much more than the words or the light they are made of. And that's what is happening here. My sons are becoming larger, more luminous, than me.

I am done trying to make sense of things. Of dead horses and wild horses, of cowboys and Indians. I am done worrying over what Avery means to our family, because I know that he brings love and nothing else. I am through trying to say that life is this or life is that, done trying to get a handle on the world so that I can present it to my sons like some carry-on bag. I want to teach them that life is more than aggression and randomness, zero and death, but words and letters are only part of it.

There are so many things I don't know about what the future holds for any of us. I may never get another chance to write my sons a letter on their birthdays, telling them how much I love them. So I will tell them now. Be strong. Be proud. Keep trying. Work hard. Go slow if you need to. Never apologize for being who you are. Don't be a victim. Remember that life is not always fair, but it is good. Success is measured by the size of your heart. Know that, in this life, you were loved as much as anyone can be loved.

I am not a hero, not even in my own story. I cannot give you that. What I can give you is the other story, this letter to you. And when I am no more, there is this: we all go on, long after we are gone, through story.

It's okay if it ends like this.

I am done.

Epilogue

Mr. Forrest Davis passed away on June 23, 2005, at the age of 83, from complications that occurred while he was on a wagon-train trip in Oregon. In his will, Mr. Davis requested that Bob Ricketts should officiate at the funeral in lieu of a clergyman. After the memorial service, Mr. Davis's casket was loaded onto a farm wagon—originally bought by his father in the early 1930s and maintained in pristine condition by Forrest over the years—and pulled to the cemetery by four Belgian draft horses that had been trained by Mr. Davis.

Acknowledgements

I am deeply indebted to a number of people who helped me with this project.

To Brant Rumble, my editor, for his encouragement and gentle humor; and to the rest of the folks at Scribner—past and present—for their hard work on my behalf.

To Gary Morris, my agent, for his wise counsel and endless patience.

To Bob Ricketts, feather-pusher and friend, for making this book happen.

To my parents, Don and Joyce Groneberg, for their continued love and support.

And to Jennifer and the boys, for everything that can't be put into words.

About the Author

Tom Groneberg is the author of *The Secret Life of Cowboys* and has written for a number of publications, including *Men's Journal*, *Big Sky Journal*, *Out*, and *Sports Afield*. Tom grew up in the suburbs of Chicago, graduated from the University of Illinois at Urbana-Champaign, and then moved west, where he worked on a number of ranches. Tom's first book, *The Secret Life of Cowboys*, received an Honor Award from the Montana Book Awards. Tom lives in northwest Montana with his wife, three sons, and his horse, Blue.